FAITH IN THE LIVING GOD

To
The Faculty of Divinity, University of Cambridge
and
The Theologische Fakultät der Universität Heidelberg

FAITH IN THE LIVING GOD

A Dialogue

JOHN POLKINGHORNE

and

MICHAEL WELKER

FORTRESS PRESS
MINNEAPOLIS

FAITH IN THE LIVING GOD

First Fortress Press edition 2001

The Scripture passages quoted by John Polkinghorne
are from The Revised Standard Version of the Bible © 1971;
those quoted by Michael Welker are the author's own translation.

ISBN 0-8006-3434-9

Printed in Great Britain

CONTENTS

INTRODUCTION

JOHN POLKINGHORNE and MICHAEL WELKER

The idea for this book arose from the experience of spending a semester together in Heidelberg in the summer of 1999. We taught a joint course concerned with central topics in Christian doctrine, and enjoyed intelligent discussions with a lively group of students. In our conversations, we found that we had enough in common in the way of belief and theological concern to find a ground on which to meet, and enough by way of difference in background and approach to make the mutual encounter challenging and illuminating for us. We want now to share with others, at one remove so to speak, this exploratory exercise, in the hope that the binocular vision that we may provide from our twin perspectives will yield helpful insight in relation to the important issues we are seeking to discuss. If there is fruitfulness here, it arises precisely from the combination of difference and commonality that we have in our interactions together.

Differences

Age and family

[J.P.] As we write, I am in my seventieth year, retired, and with a family that includes nine grandchildren. Born before the Second World War, I was a schoolboy during it and my brother, an RAF pilot, was killed in action. The biggest division among those alive today relates to people who have had direct experience of combat, with all the courage, compassion, savagery and sadness that war brings, and people who have not. Both authors are in that second cohort which has had no direct experience of war, but even at second hand and in the innocence of youth, living through those intense years of global conflict has no doubt

[1]

made its mark on the characters of those who, like me, are old enough for that to have been part of their life.

[**M.W.**] I am in the beginning of my fifties. My wife and I have twelve-year-old twin daughters. My three younger brothers and I spent our childhood in West Berlin in a very protective family, but with ruins around the house and many people in our environment physically and psychically injured by the war and the Third Reich. When I was eight I crossed the border between West and East Berlin three or four times a week to sing in the State and Cathedral choir in East Berlin. At the age of eleven I entered the French gymnasium and experienced the joy of a cosmopolitan spirit. Another formative phase was the late sixties when I was a student in Heidelberg and Tübingen, with the spirit of revolt and criticism and the hunger to renew post-war culture.

Church and culture

[**J.P.**] I am an Anglican from birth, having grown up in a Christian home. In middle life, I trained for the ministry of the Church of England and was ordained priest in 1982. Anglicans like to think that they base their theological thinking on the 'tripod' of Scripture, tradition and reason. They have always sought to have an appreciative but not uncritical relationship with general human culture, and in England they have enjoyed a special relationship with national life, resulting from the Church's establishment. The kind of interactive exchange between the scientific world view and the theological world view that has been my principal intellectual concern over the last twenty years is a kind of activity very congenial to the Anglican mind. The way in which that activity might be conducted has also been influenced by my Englishness, for my country has a pragmatic tradition and in its general intellectual life has tended to assign a relatively modest role to philosophy, in striking contrast to the German scene. In consequence, English theological thinking has been inclined to eschew laying great emphasis on methodological issues, or the construction of grand syntheses. Its focus has tended to be on discrete and particular topics.

[**M.W.**] I grew up in the churches of Berlin and Palatinate which combine Lutheran and Reformed heritage. Although my family lived only a low-profile bourgeois Protestant religiosity, as early as the age of four I wanted to become a pastor. This intention never changed till I entered the university, although I, like most of my friends, went through very church-critical phases in my life. I grew up more with French and American literature than with strong connections to the German traditions. In my student days, however, the philosophy of German Idealism of the late eighteenth and the early nineteenth centuries, and dialectical theology, a German-speaking theological movement in the 1920s and 1930s, gained my strong interest. My thinking went through 'the subjectivist turn', a concentration on human subjectivity and its epistemological potentials and the self-secularization of religion connected with it.

Education and profession

[**J.P.**] I was educated at Cambridge University, where originally I studied mathematics and where most of my academic career has been spent. After a Ph.D. in theoretical physics, I worked as a theoretical elementary particle physicist from 1955 to 1979, becoming Professor of Mathematical Physics at Cambridge in 1968 and a Fellow of the Royal Society in 1974. This long career in fundamental physics has undoubtedly formed my intellectual stance and influenced my subsequent engagement with theology. The latter approach I have often characterized as being that of a 'bottom-up thinker', meaning by that phrase one who seeks to move from experience to understanding, from the specific to the general, and who is wary of enunciating broad principles whose rooting in particularity is not obvious. Although I recognize that I am not a professional theologian in the same sense that I was a professional physicist, I have always been especially interested in New Testament studies, seeing in this discipline access to the foundational record from which Christian theology ultimately derives.

[**M.W.**] At the University of Heidelberg, where I later received a DrPhil., I studied particularly Old Testament, some church history and philosophy. In Tübingen I concentrated on systematic theology and New Testament. Here I received a DrTheol. and experienced a considerable change of my thinking when I decided to write my *Habilitationsschrift* (a post-doctoral degree needed in Germany in order to enter an academic career) on the Cambridge mathematician, natural scientist and philosopher Alfred North Whitehead. In 1977 I went to America to study Whitehead's work, almost unknown in Germany in those days, and the so-called process theology, which is shaped by Whitehead's thinking. Yet I did not become a Whiteheadian or a Process Theologian; I saw rather that Whitehead had developed a new type of thinking, as some other great theorists, particularly coming out of Harvard, had done with and after him: a multi-systemic theory which acknowledges that we approach the world with common sense, religious thought, theories shaped by the mathematical sciences, historical, ethical and other modes of thought. A general theory, according to Whitehead, does not only have to look for relative commonalities between these modes of thought, but it also has to explain their differences.

Audiences and primary partners in dialogue

[**J.P.**] I write at a variety of levels and seek to do so with intellectual care and seriousness. I am particularly anxious to write in ways that will be accessible and helpful to an open enquirer who is exploring the question of the reasonableness of Christian belief, especially if that enquirer is someone for whom scientific insight is important, or who suspects that there might be some inherent opposition between science and theology. In common with a number of other scientist-theologians, I often emphasize what I perceive as being a cousinly relationship between science and theology, in that both believe that there is a truth to be sought, whose attainment will result from the scrupulous pursuit of motivated belief.

[**M.W.**] Working on my first three academic books and beyond, I immersed myself in the theory languages of Kant, Fichte, Hegel, Schleiermacher, Nietzsche, Whitehead and Luhmann for at least one to two years each. This for a long time shaped my writings, which were primarily for academic audiences. Ironically the serious discourse with scientists which I entered into ten years ago made it necessary to transform philosophical theory language. I also became convinced that the crisis of Christianity in the West with its processes of self-secularization and self-banalization cannot be adequately addressed by theologians who are not willing to learn and to translate theory languages of the past.

Commonalities

In our concern for an interdisciplinary academic discourse which does not rest in itself but serves the Church and the oecumene of faith traditions as well as secular culture, we discovered many commonalities in the midst of the differences just described.

For both of us it is crucial not to confuse faith in the living God with fascination by a figure of thought or a great idea and the correlated certainties and intellectual and aesthetic satisfactions that go with them. Although we have both been trained in several theory languages, we seek the topical adequacy of these languages and are eager to translate them, first for each other and then for audiences which have not been trained in philosophy or in the sciences. Although we treasure the synthesizing and discriminating powers of these theory languages, we are sceptical about various forms of reductionism and types of metaphysics which do not test their figures of thought with inductive modes of thinking. We both emphatically reject the opinion that religion and theology are just culturally manipulated discourses that do not respect rationality and do not possess a consistency that is subject to evaluation. We are convinced that faith should always seek understanding and that religious convictions and certainties have to be ready to warrant truth claims.

We both believe that if Christian faith is to command respect and acceptance, it needs to be rich and detailed in its content and expression. For both of us, Trinitarian theology has this requisite 'thickness', and we seek to explain and defend this point of view in the course of the discussions that follow. As the readers will see, we are both very respectful of Scripture, though we recognize that it always requires interpretation, an activity in which the insights of contemporary understanding have an important, but by no means totally determinative, role to play. We wish to place ourselves in a consonant relationship with the tradition of the Church, while recognizing that each generation has to make that tradition its own, in its own way and in the light of its own particular situation and experience.

The Structure of the Project

The concrete project is for each author first to discuss his understanding of the threefold pillars of Christian doctrine: faith in God the creator, faith in Christ, faith in the Holy Spirit. Then each comments on the other's contribution and finally each responds briefly to the comments made on his own essay. In this way, differences and commonalities are explored dialogically and in relation to many specific topics. We both feel that the resulting bipolar treatment offers something that neither of us could have provided writing solely on his own.

The first part of the exercise completed, each then writes, in Part II, a particular essay in which his own approach is subjected to further discussion and analysis. For both authors, the question of truth is paramount in theology and so they conclude with a joint account of how truth-seeking communities may further their search for understanding, pursued in the widest setting that is possible for them.

Acknowledgements

There are many persons and many institutions who made our co-operation during the last years possible. We want to thank the Center of Theological Inquiry in Princeton, particularly its directors Dr Daniel Hardy and Dr Wallace Alston, who invited us to join and finally to chair the consultation between scientists and theologians. We thank the Alexander von Humboldt-Stiftung which offered a *Forschungspreis* to John Polkinghorne, and the Rektor of the University of Heidelberg for his hospitality. We are grateful to the more than twenty Heidelberg students who took the course 'Crucial Topics in Theology' in 1999, even though it took place on Friday afternoons and was in English only. We are also grateful to a large group of European doctoral students and colleagues for stimulating discourses on the relation of science and theology in the Internationales Wissenschaftsforum Heidelberg and at the Akademie Hofgeismar. We thank the Stiftung Volkwagen-Werk, the Hanns-Lilje-Stiftung and the Deutsche Forschungsgemeinschaft, who supported several conferences, which led to further publications beyond this enterprise. Finally, we are grateful for the technical support that Beate Müller and Wolfram Kerner gave us when we prepared the manuscript for publication.

This book has emerged out of a dialogue over seven years and the personal and theological friendship whose fruits we now offer to truth-seeking communities in the Church, the academy and the theologically open and interested wider cultural public.

PART I

FAITH IN THE LIVING GOD

1

FAITH IN GOD THE CREATOR

JOHN POLKINGHORNE

All three significant words of the title can trip up a scientist. We shall consider these *skandala* (stones of stumbling) in turn.

Faith

'Faith' can readily conjure up the image of blind belief in really rather incredible propositions that are presented for unquestioning acceptance on the sole basis of an unquestionable authority. This misconception is perhaps the biggest barrier that has to be surmounted by a scientist with an inclination to look into religious matters. Naturally, such a person does not wish to commit intellectual suicide, but all too easily they can suppose that this is what is being asked of them. The idea that faith might be concerned with the search for understanding (as Anselm said in the Middle Ages) will often be a novel concept for scientists. This misconception about the nature of faith has arisen for a number of reasons.

One is simply the failure to recognize that religious believers have motivations for their beliefs. The whole discipline of apologetics is concerned with seeking to articulate these motivations in a way that will be helpful to an enquirer. This activity is not just the sugar-coating of a bitter fideistic pill that has to be swallowed whole, but it is a genuine attempt to express the reasonable origins of religious faith. I have written books seeking to explain and defend my scientific beliefs in quantum theory and in the role of quarks and gluons as the constituents of nuclear matter,[1] and I have also written books seeking to explain and defend my Christian belief.[2] Although the material is very different in these two sets of writings, the underlying strategy is the same. In each case one has to tell a complex story of interlocking experience and interpretation that has developed within a truth-seeking community, not without the struggles, perplexities and setbacks that are common to human intellectual endeavour. At the same time, one has to convey concepts that are radically different from those of everyday common sense. No one can understand quantum theory who is unwilling to accept the necessity of revisionary thinking. It would be unreasonable to expect that enquiry into the divine would prove free from comparable intellectual surprise.

But, the enquiring scientist might say, is not the material in fact so different in these two exercises that one is seen to be a rational enquiry, while the other amounts, in the end, to no more than dependence on irrational assertion? The issue of the nature of revelation is then put onto the agenda, raising the question of what it is that religious people are appealing to when they make use of 'revelation' as the basis of their motivation to believe. It might seem that we have returned to an appeal to unchallengeable authority, for many of those who stumble at the word revelation do so because they believe that it refers to infallible propositions uttered *ex cathedra Dei*. Certainly, a concise statement like the Nicene Creed does seem to have an air of categorical assertiveness about it. But so also do the particle data tables that high energy physicists carry around in their pockets. Both are distillations of the essence of complex interactions between experience and interpretation. In the case of scientific knowledge, the experiences are experiments, that is to say, carefully contrived occasions on which some particular aspect of natural process will be most perspicuously discernible. Because experiments are the results of human manipulation, they represent experience that is repeatable, giving it, at least in principle, a universal accessibility. For the Christian believer, in addition to his or her individual religious experience, the prime motivations for faith are the foundational events of the tradition in which God's will and nature are believed to have been most clearly discerned, through the history of Israel and in the person of Jesus Christ. These events were graciously given by God and so they are unique and they have to be accepted or rejected in their unavoidable uniqueness. Those sciences that have an historical dimension are not totally unfamiliar with the givenness of the unique. Evolutionary biology has only one history of terrestrial life on which to base its insights; cosmology only one universe to study.

There is certainly a significant degree of difference at this point between scientific belief and religious belief, but an appeal to the unique is by no means to be understood as an irrational move. Justifying that claim requires some account of the nature of rational thought. I believe that its essence lies in a seeking to conform our thinking to the nature of the object of our thought. Behind that claim there obviously lies a realist stance in relation to human epistemological and ontological abilities; in other words, a trust that what we know is a reliable guide to what is actually the case. I do not believe that we are lost in a Kantian fog, out of which loom the phenomenal shadows of inaccessible noumena, so that we know only appearances and not things as they are. Here, at least, scientists are unlikely to find much difficulty, for they are almost all, consciously or unconsciously, realists about their encounter with the physical world. I have sought elsewhere to defend a critical realism in both science and theology,[3] and I shall not pursue the general point further on this occasion. Realism is, however, fundamental to the exercise on which we are engaged. Just as I do not accept a pragmatist account of science that would see its primary concern as the achievement of technological success, so I do not accept an account of religious faith that regards it as primarily furnishing a technique for living. Just as I do not accept a social constructivist account of science (while not failing to acknowledge the role played by the community in the enterprise of science), so I do not accept an account of religious faith that regards it primarily as a cultural binding force in society. I believe that both science and religion are concerned with knowing and responding to the way things actually are, though neither of them has access to simple, direct and unproblematic knowledge of the unseen realities of which they seek to speak, nor absolute certainty about the validity of the insights they attain. Critical realism is the attempt to find a middle way between the heroic optimism of the failed modernist search for certain truth, and the intellectual pessimism that so often leads postmodernism into a slough of relativistic despond.

Even within science itself, we can see that rationality in the sense we have been discussing does not take a single universal form. The diversity of reality prevents this from being so. The quantum world has an entirely different character from that of the everyday world of Newtonian physics. Not only is the quantum world cloudy, so that Heisenberg's uncertainty principle denies us exhaustively clear knowledge of its process, but also its relationships are such that a special quantum logic applies to them,[4] different from the classical logic of Aristotle and everyday life. Quantum entities have to be known on their own terms and in accordance with their idiosyncratic rationality. It would scarcely be surprising if similar considerations applied to knowledge of the divine.

Failure to acknowledge this point, together with a simplistic notion that science deals in plain 'facts' (despite it being clear that there are no interesting scientific facts that are not already interpreted facts[5]), has often led scientists to a narrow and unsatisfactory identification of the reasonable with what is thinkable within the limited protocols of scientific argument. Many popular books about science are garnished with a broad-brush kind of intellectual history in which the rise of the sun of science is portrayed as dispelling the irrational mists of an age of faith. The idea that thinkers like Augustine or Aquinas were deficient in reason – or in an interest in the science of their time, for that matter – is a very curious belief. Of course, they were people of their age, with the opportunities and limitations that implied, just as were the precursors of modern science, such as Roger Bacon and Nicholas Oresme, usually given a more sympathetic treatment. One of the benefits that scientific reason acquires from the impersonal repeatability of experiment is that its understanding is cumulative in character. At the beginning of the twenty-first century, an ordinary scientist knows and understands a great deal that was hidden even from the geniuses in 1900. Scientists, in consequence, live in the intellectual present. Theology, together with all other forms of human rational enquiry operating at the level of the personal, has always to engage in dialogue across the centuries in order to avoid the distortions and limitations that would be imposed on its deep and many-faceted encounter with reality by a purely contemporary perspective. Theologians have to live within a historical tradition.

God

The second word at which a scientist might stumble is 'God'. Two contrasting pitfalls lie in the way. One is the concept of the invisible Magician who from time to time tinkers with the natural process of the universe in a capricious way. Needless to say, such a notion is *theologically* incredible. The God who is worthy of worship must be consistent and faithful. 'Shall not the Judge of all the earth do right?' (Genesis 18.25). The Ordainer of the laws of nature will not be an arbitrary interferer with them. A surprising number of scientists, however, seem to suppose that it is just such a magical deity in whom they are being invited to believe. In a recent debate, the Nobel Prize winner and staunch atheist Steven Weinberg said that there could be evidence for a God. As an example he suggested the sudden appearance of a flaming sword that decapitated him, the unbeliever. I replied that were so bizarre and unfortunate an incident to happen, it would cause me the greatest theological difficulty, because of its capricious and irrational character.

It would be disingenuous, however, not to recognize that the Old Testament sometimes seems to portray God as acting in just that kind of way (for example, Exodus 4.24–6), and that some of the tragic happenings of human life might also seem to suggest a God of this trickster character. It is the task of theology, through exegesis and theodicy, to wrestle with these perplexities and to seek to resolve them. It is not possible to pursue these important issues in detail here, nor to claim that were this to be done the apparent problems would easily be solved. The Bible cannot be treated as uniformly inspired and authoritative in all its utterance. Principles of interpretation have to be worked out that acknowledge that its human writings contain both eternal truths and also many matters that are the deposits of historical and cultural particularity and limitation. The long tale of human misery and suffering has also to be treated with the most profound seriousness. It is precisely as it struggles with these difficult issues that theology manifests itself as being a truth-seeking and rational form of human enquiry.

An alternative error about the nature of God would be to use the word simply as a cypher for the rational order of the universe. This seems to have been what Einstein did. His general writings contain a number of often quoted aphorisms about the divine, but he explained more than once that he did not believe in a personal God, but thought of himself as a follower of Spinoza, whose characteristic phrase was *deus sive natura*, equating God and nature. This kind of usage is quite common in contemporary popular books about science. The cynical will say that, following the astounding success of Stephen Hawking's *A Brief History of Time*, with its recurrent and somewhat inconsistent invocation of the Mind of God, authors have come to believe that such a tactic is good for sales. Others might see here a certain wistful but wary concern with the possibility of a deeper level of meaning than that to which science, by itself, can give access. The very persistence with which the question of God continues to exercise many minds, even those of avowed atheists, could be interpreted as evidence for a suppressed but continuing *sensus Dei*. No doubt there is some truth in both these interpretations.

Theologically, however, this concept of God is far too thin to be satisfactory. It does not do much work and so many may be tempted to think that they might just as well take the order of the universe as being a brute fact in itself. It is the purpose of what follows to explore whether there are reasonable grounds for belief in a creator God that can support an altogether richer concept of the divine.

Creator

Our final stone of stumbling is the word 'creator' itself. No theological misconception is more widespread in the scientific community, or more of a hindrance to a fruitful engagement between science and theology, than that the role of the creator is simply to start things off. One classic expression of this error is Hawking's celebrated and naive observation that if the universe had no datable beginning (as his speculative cosmological theory supposes), then there would be nothing left for a creator to do.[6] Of course, the doctrine of creation is concerned not with temporal beginning, but with ontological origin. People seem to divide into two classes according to how they regard the question 'Why is there something rather than nothing?' For some it raises a deep and important issue; for others it is an unintelligible or uninteresting enquiry. It is the former who are seized of the question of the existence of a creator.

The implication of what has been said so far is that the nature of faith is that it is a commitment and response to the real. When faith seeks understanding (to use again Anselm's celebrated definition of the theological task), it is concerned with the exploration of the nature of reality. Whether that quest is fittingly seen as being exploration into God the creator will depend critically upon the scope and character of what is considered to make up reality. A leaden reductionist physicalism will be too earthbound to allow the possibility of a glance heavenwards. Science's own success in its own domain must not be allowed to impose upon us the assumption that there alone is to be found all that is worthy of rational enquiry. Absolutely no one, whatever their official beliefs, actually lives their lives as if this were so, for human personality is richer than so desiccated an account could ever encompass. The reality to which faith seeks to respond must be generously and adequately construed, so that it accommodates not only what we might write about in the abstraction of our studies, but also that by which we live in the profound complexity of our active engagement with the way things are.

Of central importance will be how the human encounter with value is to be understood. What is the nature of our ethical intuitions? Is the statement that torturing children is wrong some sort of veiled strategy for evolutionary effectiveness (it might be more useful to put them to work as slaves), or a socially constructed attitude (a convention of our society), or a fact about the way things are (so that there is genuine moral knowledge, which, in its own way, is as much about reality as scientific knowledge is about its particular aspect of reality)? A similar question may be asked about our aesthetic experiences. Do they derive from a veiled recognition of situations favourable to survival, or are they simply biochemical consequences of the emission of certain neurotransmitters in the brain, or are they indispensable and irreducible insights into the nature of a world that is charged with intrinsic beauty? To be honest, one must also add, what is the status of experiences of ugliness and terror? Are they signs of a hostile or indifferent reality, or the consequences of a fallen world marred by a disastrous ancestral act, or signals of the presence of a malevolent or ambiguous deity, or what?

Three things may be said in answer to these questions. The first is that they certainly refer to realms of experience that are culturally influenced in their character. The moral corruption of certain societies (Hitler and Stalin), the tales that the anthropologists bring back, the recurrent aesthetic crises in which a generation initially rejects the artistic developments of its own pioneers, all make that clear enough. Science itself, being the activity of a community, is not unfamiliar with this kind of effect. Without accepting all that Thomas Kuhn had to say about revolutionary periods in science,[7] one can agree that often a new paradigm triumphs partly because of the death of its older opponents. (Poincaré and Lorentz, great men though they were, never fully came to terms with the interpretation that the young Einstein had given of the equations that they had correctly formulated, but whose real import they had not fully comprehended.) Yet, the presence of cultural tricks of perspective, whether in ethics, art or science, does not imply that nothing of reality is discernible from that point of view. It simply encourages us to a degree of caution in its assessment.

The second point to make is that though science is often regarded as being officially 'value free' (so that the editors of The Physical Review would not pass an argument simply alleging that this is the way that things ought to be), nevertheless, within the community of practising scientists, the acknowledgement of value plays an important role.[8] This is not simply because of the honesty and generosity that are required in any truth-seeking community, but also because, in their informal and heuristic discussions, scientists are often guided to discoveries through following principles of value, such as economy and elegance and the search for beautiful equations. This is a point to which we shall return.

A third, and most important, point is that how the status of value is regarded is fundamental to any metaphysical enterprise, such as the exploration of faith in God the creator. Many scientists – Jacques Monod[9] and Steven Weinberg[10] would be particularly distinguished examples – have a humane respect for the kind of personally perceived values that we have been discussing, but they also believe them simply to be expressions of individually or communally constructed attitudes. For such people, our ethical stances and aesthetic experiences are internal to the world of human culture, constituting a little island of self-generated meaning from which we heroically defy the ocean of cosmic hostility and meaninglessness that laps about us. We are simply what we choose to make of ourselves. 'The ancient covenant is in pieces; man at last knows that he is alone in the unfeeling immensity of the universe, out of which he emerged by chance.'[11] There is a certain stoic nobility in this attitude, but I believe it to be fundamentally mistaken. Instead I believe that our ethical intuitions and aesthetic delights are windows through which we truly look onto a rich realm of created reality, within which the creator has set us and which extends far beyond the world of human-generated thoughts and attitudes.

Perspectives on Reality

Of course, as we approach these windows, we shall often find that some of them are dirty and their glass distorting. If there is real moral knowledge, as I believe there to be, we are not in perfect possession of it. The corruptions of moral judgement that are present in individual lives and within the varied histories of society make that only too clear. A degree of corrective can be found within the moral tradition of a community, but communities are not themselves immune from serious ethical distortion. Two observations may be made. One is the sad fact that terrible deeds are often done for ostensibly 'good' reasons (for example the error of attempting forced religious conversions). Though we can see retrospectively the dreadful mistakes that were made in this way, there was some kind of appeal to morality, though of a hideously corrupted kind. The second observation is of the existence of a kind of ethical immuno-suppressive system, whereby there is a counter-reaction within a community to the presence of moral infection (the Franciscans at the time of the crusades; the Confessing Church in Nazi Germany). Similarly, we must acknowledge that the power of the arts can be used both for human flourishing and for human degradation.

To explore and defend the claim that reality is value-laden is fundamental to the exploration and defence of faith in God the creator. The belief that this enquiry motivates is much more than a vague sense of being at home in the universe. It will achieve its credibility through its detailed content and the richness and comprehensiveness of its explanatory scope.

The quest on which we are embarked is metaphysical in its character. Here is another word at which the scientist may stumble. Metaphysics is concerned with the attainment of a world view, but if that view is rightly to deserve the noble epithet 'metaphysical' it will have to strive for the integration of many domains of human knowledge, respecting their proper insights, and even their seeming differences and clashes, while seeking a true synthesis of the whole.

In the vocabulary of the scientific community, 'metaphysical' often carries as pejorative a tone as does its companion word 'theological'. Yet the way in which the writers of popular books on science delight in practising the metaphysical art (as when an author slides from science to scientism by pretending that the only questions to ask or answer are scientific) makes it clear that it is as natural to have a metaphysics as it is to speak prose. The point to strive for is adequacy to the complexity of reality, eschewing a trivial synthesis obtained through Procrustean truncation.

In this task, it is important to recognize that science constrains metascience but it does not determine it. The point is easily illustrated from within physics. Causality is a metaphysical issue. Is quantum theory indeterministic? Niels Bohr says 'Yes'; David Bohm says 'No'.[12] Their conflicting interpretations have identical empirical consequences but radically different accounts of the nature of reality. Unaided science cannot adjudicate between them. Criteria for metaphysical choice include economy, elegance and wide scope. In the case of the Bohr/Bohm controversy, it is the feeling that Bohm's clever ideas have about them an unattractive air of contrivance that is one of the main reasons why almost all physicists who think seriously about the matter have sided with Bohr.

In terms of the metaphor of windows onto reality, the crucial metaphysical issue of scope can be expressed in terms of the number of different windows through which we look, and whose perspectives we seek to combine in forming our understanding of the multi-dimensional landscape that we encounter. Reductionist scientism is a one-window view, whose flat portrayal neglects all that is of value and significance in our personal lives. The obverse metaphysical stance is one whose windows are only those that open into the interior human self. René Descartes' appeal to the certainty of the thinking ego, as the basis on which to build reliable knowledge, had this character. This heroic bid for clear and certain ideas has proved a failure. We have to recognize that there is an irreducible degree of precariousness involved in the metaphysical enterprise. There is no Archimedean point from which we can survey reality with complete neutrality; no window that does not impose its own perspective. No one has access to knock-down knowledge.

I shall be arguing for a monotheistic metaphysics, but I do not pretend for a moment that my atheist friends are simply stupid not to see it my way. However, I do believe that Christian monotheism explains more than atheism, that it provides the most satisfactory reconciliation of the views from the widest range of windows to which we have access. We have to use all the resources for inspecting reality that are available to us, for the only way to reduce the chance of perspectival error is to make use of as multi-ocular a vision as possible. The transcendental method of Immanuel Kant was another great metaphysical attempt to be sparing in the use of windows. The fact that we now know that Euclidean geometry is not an *a priori* category but a serviceable empirical approximation encourages us to make full use of those scientific windows that look out on the physical world and that Kant was not inclined to employ.

We must also recognize that from time to time people of genius enlarge our view by opening a new window, or cleaning one that had become obscured, so that we gain better access to the metaphysical landscape. The insights of Freud, Jung and other depth psychologists may be the subject of controversy and contention, but they have made us aware of the existence of unconscious depths and motivations within the human self which must be taken into account in forming an adequate picture of the nature of the personal, since that picture has to go beyond the thoughts and feelings of which we are immediately aware.

In my view, the strategy to be pursued is one that takes with all due seriousness all the perspectives that are available to us in our encounter with reality. I wish now briefly to draw attention to a number of metaphysical windows whose views bear upon the question of belief in God the creator.

Windows onto Reality: Light and Darkness

(1) *Cosmic order*. The window of fundamental physical science discloses a universe whose rational transparency makes science possible and whose rational beauty rewards the scientific enquirer with a profound sense of wonder.[13] In short, the cosmos is shot through with signs of mind and it is an attractive, though not inevitable, thought that it is indeed the mind of the creator that is partially disclosed in this way. While we have already rejected the notion of God as functioning solely as a cypher for cosmic order, nevertheless the fact of that order can properly form part of a cumulative case for theistic belief.

(2) *Cosmic fruitfulness*. The much-discussed insights of the Anthropic Principle[14] make it clear that the early universe was already pregnant with the possibility of carbon-based life billions of years before its actual emergence, in that the forces of nature, as we experience them, are 'finely tuned' to have just that character and those intrinsic strengths that alone would enable the possibility of the long and delicately balanced chain of circumstances, both terrestrial and astrophysical, that have led to life on Earth. The slightest change in the detailed constitution of these forces would have rendered the universe boring and sterile in its history.

Further insights into cosmic fruitfulness may be emerging from the discoveries of the infant science of complexity theory. At present heavily dependent upon the study of computer models, this new discipline shows that complex systems are capable of spontaneously generating astonishing degrees of holistic order in their overall behaviour. Stuart Kauffman has suggested that phenomena of this kind may have played a significant role in the evolution of life, in addition to the effects of natural selection.[15] If this is the case, many of the basic structures that comparative anatomists note in the forms of living beings may be ahistorical necessities, rather than the deposit of historical contingency, as conventional neo-Darwinism supposes.

These scientific insights sit comfortably with the theistic understanding that the purpose of the creator lies behind the unfolding history of the universe, without, of course, constituting a conclusive proof that this is so. In particular, theology need feel no anxiety as science reveals more of the structure-generating power of the laws of nature, whether realized through the shuffling explorations of natural selection or through the autopoietic properties of complex systems. The creator's will is as much expressed through the laws of nature that God ordains as it would be through any other form of divine action. This understanding helps to relieve any tension that exegetes might have felt between Genesis 1.24 ('And God said, "Let the earth bring forth living creatures ..."') and Genesis 1.25 ('And God made the beasts of the earth ...').

(3) *The dawning of consciousness.* Perhaps the most surprising and significant event of cosmic history, post-Big Bang, of which we are aware, has been the coming-to-be of self-consciousness here on Earth. In ourselves the universe has become aware of itself. As Pascal said, human beings are thinking *reeds* (acknowledging our frailty and insignificance of scale in relation to the vast universe around us), but we are *thinking* reeds, and so greater than all the stars, for we know them and ourselves and they know nothing. The monotheism of the Abrahamic faiths (on this point Judaism, Christianity and Islam are at one) does not treat this remarkable occurrence as fortuitous – a happy accident – but sees it as a very important clue to the meaning of cosmic process, a striking sign of the deep significance of the personal.

(4) *Religious experience.* At all times and in all places there have been those who testify to encounter with a transcendent reality that we may call the sacred. Often, such people have constituted a majority. It is beyond the scope of this chapter to consider in detail how one should evaluate this testimony, impressive as it is in its weight, and perplexing as it is in the cognitive clashes that there seem to be between the accounts that the different faith traditions give of their experience and of the insight that testimony conveys.[16] The theist will see behind this kaleidoscopic variety a meeting with the Reality of the divine presence. Two points may briefly be made. In addition to the experiences of the great religious leaders and prophets, and the experiences of the mystical adepts, there is the witness of the ordinary believers, those whom the Christian tradition calls the holy common people of God. Their faith is not sustained by experiences of striking and unusual character but by the diligent practice of their religion in the place of worship, in the home and in daily public life. An account of God the creator must encompass

the totality of religious experience and avoid the spiritual elitism that led William James, in *The Varieties of Religious Experience*,[17] to place perhaps too great an emphasis on the religious 'pattern setters'. The second point is to note that there is widespread witness to the self-authenticating character of this encounter with the sacred. Of course, people can be deluded, but the feeling of spiritual necessity, that 'Here I am, I can do no other' is fundamental to the religious life.

(5) *Moral evil.* Human history and individual introspection both show that there is something awry with humanity. Paul spoke for us all when he said 'I do not understand my own actions. For I do not do what I want, but I do the very thing I hate' (Romans 7.15). No metaphysical account would be adequate that did not consider seriously the existence of moral evil, the chosen cruelties and shabby compromises of human-kind. Christian theism calls this moral slantedness 'sin' and diagnoses it as due to the human exercise of God's gift of free will to produce a self-chosen isolation from the life of the creator. Christianity's understanding of human fulfilment is that it does not consist in 'doing it my way' but in the embrace of a life lived in communion with God. We have become alienated from the divine life and need to find a way of return. If this is so, the concept of God the creator has to be expanded to include the concept of God the redeemer, who reconciles us and enables our entry into a new kind of life. That spiritual experience will be one of the concerns of my next chapter, but it is important to recognize that Christian theism only attains a 'thickness' of insight sufficient to make it fully persuasive when it is considered in its Trinitarian fullness.

(6) *Physical evil.* We have already noted the serious challenge to theistic belief that is represented by the widespread incidence of disease and disaster, sometimes leading to impressive responses of spiritual fortitude, but often appearing to crush people under burdens too heavy to be borne. This problem is one of great profundity and there is no simple 'one-line' answer that a theist can give. There is, however, one small insight that combining science with the doctrine of creation can offer, and which is of some mild help. Science describes an evolving universe, whether it is recounting the history of the stars or the history of terrestrial life. Theologically, an evolutionary world can be understood as a creation allowed by its creator 'to make itself'. God could no doubt have produced a ready-made world with a snap of the divine fingers, but

the God of love does not act in so summary a fashion. Rather, the creator has endowed creation with an intrinsic fruitfulness that it can then explore and realize in its own way. One may see this creaturely self-making as constituting a great good, but it has a necessary cost. The same biochemical processes that have driven evolution by allowing some cells to mutate and so produce new forms of life must, necessarily, in a non-magic universe, allow other cells to mutate and become malignant. One cannot have the one without the other. In other words, the presence of cancer in our world is not a sign of divine callousness or incompetence. It is the necessary cost of a world allowed to make itself. The more science understands the process of the universe, the more it appears to be an interlocking 'package deal', with the 'good' and the 'bad' inextricably intertwined. In this sense, the existence of physical evil is not gratuitous, something that God could have remedied by taking a bit more trouble. Of course, many perplexities remain, but there is some modest help for theism here.

(7) *Futility*. Science tells us, most reliably, that the universe is going to die, through either collapse or decay, over a timespan of tens of billions of years, just as surely as we are going to die over a timespan of tens of years. Both realizations put in question what could be the ultimate purpose of the creator of a world of such transience. Notoriously, when Weinberg thought about the certainty of cosmic futility, he said that the more he understood the universe, the more it seemed pointless to him.[18] The challenge this poses to theism is a serious one. It makes it clear that a mere evolutionary optimism – the feeling that present process will lead to ultimate fulfilment – is an illusion. If there is a hope for true fulfilment, either for ourselves or for the whole of creation, it lies on the other side of death. Of course, Christianity believes that there is such a destiny *post mortem*, not only for human individuals but also, in some mysterious way, for the whole created order (Colossians 1.15–20). Once again we see how the metaphysical quest for total meaningfulness, if pursued in the direction of Christian theism, leads to a satisfactory response only if its theological base is appropriately rich and Trinitarian.

These windows have looked out onto a variety of landscapes, some sunny and some sombre. The beauty of the cosmic order contrasts with the messy and painful scene presented by the existence of physical evil. The fruitfulness of cosmic history to date contrasts with the certainty of eventual cosmic futility. The remarkable emergence of human consciousness has produced at the same time the human capacity for moral evil.

Despite the perplexities expressed in these contrasts, faith in the creator holds to the belief that the universe does make total sense. That faith is grounded in the conviction of the deep meaningfulness of cosmic history and the ultimate hopefulness of cosmic destiny. Such a truly all-embracing belief cannot be an absolute certainty – any more than its denial could be – but it is a motivated understanding of what we know about the richness of reality. It is a belief that countless Christian believers, including the present writers, have been prepared to embrace and to base their lives upon.

Our present discussion has been framed in terms of the metaphor of windows onto reality. Like all metaphors, it has its limitations, for it conjures up the image of a tranquil cognitive gaze directed at a passive reality. But God is not there just to be the answer to our intellectual curiosity. Faith in God affects our lives in ways that have no parallels in scientific understanding. I believe most firmly in quarks and gluons as the constituents of matter, but that belief leaves the greater part of me unaffected. Faith in God the creator does not merely make sense of the cosmos but it calls on me to accept my finite status as a creature and to respond in worshipful obedience to the divine majesty and divine will of the maker of heaven and earth.

Comments: Is There a Natural Awareness of God?
MICHAEL WELKER

I fully agree that in seeking an understanding of God we deal with reality: 'When faith seeks understanding ... it is concerned with the nature of reality.' However, as you pointed out, our understanding of reality would be distorted if only materialistic nature or scientistically defined reality were meant by this. Rather, cultural and religious reality needs to be explored when we speak of faith and of God.

My impression is that you give much more weight to the word 'faith' than to the words 'in God the Creator'. You very strongly state with what the creator should not be confused. For a positive explanation you turn to our relation to the creator and, above all, to our relation to the created reality, to the orders of creation. In my opinion, this is not only particularly helpful for those who are estranged from the language and the images of traditional faith, but also to firm believers. Both groups will appreciate your attempt to approach faith in God the creator with intellectual honesty. As in all academic work, honesty is also crucial in theological endeavours.

Those, however, who still live in the world and in the language of Christian faith may be challenged by your thoughts to ask: 'How do the "windows onto reality" direct us toward the creator?' In other words, is there something like a 'natural awareness of God'? This question has certainly been heavily disputed in the history of Christian theology. Some theologians thought that 'natural awareness' leads to a confusion of God and nature, or even to a confusion of God and the human being. With regard to this problem I have always liked Calvin's statement at the beginning of his famous Dogmatic Theology, The Institutes. *It says that there is of course a natural awareness, a 'presentiment' of the Divine. When we see all the wonders of harmony and power in cosmic, social and aesthetic realms and orders, we feel overwhelmed. But this knowledge is 'vague and fleeting'. It does not lead to a* clear *recognition of God.*

How do we access 'foundational events of the tradition of faith'?

My second question concerns what you call 'the foundational events of the tradition of faith'. We do not have access to these events in the same way in which we can refer to natural events. We have them only as witnessed to by faith, mostly in the canonic traditions of the Bible. The canonic traditions of the Bible grew over a millennium. They have their very different ways of addressing reality and its rationalities. Some of these traditions are very remote from our currently dominant rationalities and our approaches toward reality. But all of them form very subtle networks. And only in these networks of witnesses and stories are the foundational events what they are.

Am I correct in seeing here another analogy to the natural sciences? Without the tools of mathematics you do not get very far in science. And without a deep engagement with Scripture, without some sense of the canonic rationalities, it is difficult to understand the foundational events of the tradition of faith. Does this mean that a preliminary understanding of who God is and what God wants creation to live up to is always present in our look back on these events? Does this mean that the 'natural awareness' of God is more or less pre-shaped by a pre-understanding of the God revealed?

Do the 'dark sides of creation' affect our values and morals?

I was grateful to see that you do not only refer to the glorious and beautiful sides of the created order, but also to moral evil, physical evil and cosmic futility. I think that our sense for value and our moral knowledge are also shaped by these factors. Coming as I do from a country which saw totally corrupted public morals, my general concept of morals and of our relation to value seems slightly more neutral. I think that we personally and publicly live with hierarchies of values and virtues. This allows us to cope and to live with a pluralism of preferences in our communities and societies. For some people and lifeworlds, for example, prudence governs the hierarchy, although faith, love, courage and other virtues and values are not absent. For others, courage might be dominant. For still others, love, and so forth. If the top value becomes too dominant and weakens the presence of the other values and virtues, we get distortive value-systems.

Moral communication, in my understanding, is the giving and taking of respect, attention and admiration, by which we mutually control and stimulate our actions. The problem is that situations can arise in which distorted value-systems govern our morals. Then the good are called bad, and the bad are called good. Faith addresses these pressing situations with its understanding of 'sin'. The Lord's Prayer addresses these problems by asking God to 'not lead us into temptation' and to 'deliver us from evil'. In modernity we have lost perspectives on this dimension. In my view you could bring this syndrome even more to the fore.

Reply: Knowledge of God
JOHN POLKINGHORNE

More weight given to faith (and its possible grounds) than to God, the object of faith? Here the limitations of a bottom-up approach are beginning to be exposed; the vulnerability of natural theology, pursued on its own, exhibited. Of course that kind of knowledge of God is liable to prove 'vague and fleeting' if that is all there is to say. Yet if there were not at least that much to say, would not knowledge of God seem abstract and assertive? The truth of the matter is that we need all the resources we can in that great quest for knowledge of the divine. It would be strange indeed if there were no hints of deity to be seen in what is claimed to be created nature; stranger still if that were the whole story.

Bottom-up thinking, with its appeal to experience, cannot be wholly independent of a top-down interpretative framework within which to understand that experience, any more than a mature science can operate outside a subtle and complex network of principles and phenomena, interlocked in mutually illuminative interaction. In respect of both science and theology, I would agree that 'only in these networks of witnesses and stories are the foundational events what they are'. Hence the indispensable role that thinking within a tradition plays in both disciplines, as indispensable as thinking conducted under the spur of experience, both one's own and that reliably reported to one.

We cannot but perceive reality from a perspective, with all the dangers and opportunities that implies. I agree about the particular dangers of moral distortion and I believe that in the widest dialogue with others, and not only those who are our contemporaries, lies our best hope of finding necessary challenge and correction.

NOTES

1. J. C. Polkinghorne, *The Quantum World*, Longman/Princeton University Press, 1984; *Rochester Roundabout*, Longman/W. H. Freeman, 1989.
2. J. C. Polkinghorne, *The Way the World Is*, Triangle/Eerdmans, 1983; *Science and Christian Belief/The Faith of a Physicist*, SPCK/Princeton University Press, 1994.
3. J. C. Polkinghorne, *Rochester Roundabout*, ch. 21; *Reason and Reality*, SPCK/Trinity Press International, 1991, chs 1 and 2; *Beyond Science*, Cambridge University Press, 1996, ch. 2; *Belief in God in an Age of Science*, Yale University Press, 1998, chs 2 and 5.
4. The superposition principle allows the addition of A and not-A to produce a middle term undreamed of by Aristotle; see Polkinghorne, *Quantum World*, ch. 3.
5. See note 1.
6. S. W. Hawking, *A Brief History of Time*, Bantam, 1988, p. 141.
7. T. Kuhn, *The Structure of Scientific Revolutions*, Chicago University Press, 1970.
8. Polkinghorne, *Beyond Science*, ch. 8.
9. J. Monod, *Chance and Necessity*, Collins, 1972.
10. S. Weinberg, *Dreams of a Final Theory*, Hutchinson, 1993, ch. 11.
11. Monod, *Chance and Necessity*, p. 167.
12. See, for instance, Polkinghorne, *Quantum World*, chs 6 and 8.

13. See note 8.
14. See, for instance, J. Leslie, *Universes*, Routledge, 1989.
15. S. Kauffman, *At Home in the Universe*, Oxford University Press, 1995.
16. See Polkinghorne, *Christian Belief/Faith*, ch. 10.
17. W. James, *The Varieties of Religious Experience*, Collins, 1960.
18. S. Weinberg, *The First Three Minutes*, A. Deutsch, 1977, p. 149.

2

FAITH IN GOD THE CREATOR

MICHAEL WELKER

Faith in God the creator is not the more or less vague idea that there is some foundation of the world, some beginning of the universe, some power which in the first second of the universe or beyond it was at work. Faith in God the creator is *a living and trusting relationship to the shaping, judging and saving power; to the personal will which keeps together nature, culture and history, and in all this, our lives; and to the personal instance which directs the creaturely being and life and gives it its meaning, direction and destination.*

The God Who Created Me: Strength and Danger of the Existentialist Reduction

Faith means becoming familiar with this God, becoming acquainted with this God, or in biblical terms, *to search for God and to love God.* By the search for God no religious game of hide-and-seek is meant, but the persistent striving for an ever clearer awareness and knowledge of God, for a deeper revelation of God and the divine will among us. To love God does not mean a romantic being in love with another individual or a mystical absorption into an abyss of a reality that cannot be known, but to love God means to keep God's commandments, to accept God's revelation, to discover and to treasure God's intentions for the creation, to be ready and willing to engage in these interests and to work for them on this earth and in its history.[1]

Faith in the creator engrosses the whole human existence. It gives a direction, a weight, a dignity to human life, which a fixed 'ultimate point', a highest idea or a principal natural law could not possibly provide. The Reformer Martin Luther attempted to grasp this engaged faith relation by emphasizing in his explanation of the creed that 'I believe in God the creator' means that I believe that God created *me*.[2] However, as Luther is well aware, the important relation to 'myself' and 'the I' must not be seen isolated from the rest of creation.

He states: '"I believe in God the Father almighty, creator of heaven and earth." What does this mean? Answer: I believe that God has created me *together with all creatures*.' The concentration on the single person and on myself is good and important on the one hand, because it grasps faith as a living *personal* relationship to God. It makes sense because it aims at expressing God's caring goodness, God's love for the creatures. On the other hand it is problematic because it is very strongly concentrated on the human being (anthropocentric) and very strongly directed towards the single I (egocentric).

Many theologians, though they meant to follow Luther, reduced faith to the inner relationship of the abstract 'I' or 'the inner self' to God, or rather what they took to be 'God'. They thus often propagated a very abstract and empty notion of creation and faith, a 'relation of the origin to my existence' or similarly dry metaphysical figures of thought. Luther himself is not in this danger of empty abstraction. In his *Small Catechism* (written above all for the uneducated and for the children) he does not only state that God created me 'with all creatures'. He explains this in detail. I believe that God 'has given me and still sustains my body and soul, eyes and ears and all my limbs, my reason and all the senses, also clothing and shoes, food and drink, house and home, wife and child, field, cattle and all property; that he provides me abundantly and daily with all the necessities and the nourishment of body and life, protects me from all danger and preserves me from all evil'.[3]

With this, a very concrete spectrum of the divine creativity and a very broad spectrum of God's creative activity comes into view. Luther's *Large Catechism* widens the perspective even more by emphasizing that God gives us 'sun, moon and stars in the sky, day and night, air, fire, water, the earth and everything it produces, birds, fish, animals, grain, and all kinds of plants. He also gives us all the other good things we have on earth: good government, peace, security.'[4] Thus we realize that God the creator is not only 'my God', but the Lord of nature, culture, history and of the powers of heaven and earth. Again, God is not just an 'all-synthesizing Subject', but a loving, justifying, judging and saving power, will and personal instance. It is only in this differentiation that we reach the level of the biblical witnesses.

'I believe in God the creator.' This statement expresses a very comprehensive relationship of trust in the creative will, in the creative power, in the creative personal instance which directs and rules nature, culture, history and, in them, our lives. Some theologians therefore called faith a 'trust that founds existence', which, however, should not get confused with the idea that human trust itself can be regarded as founding existence. Quite the contrary, faith in the creator is a trust in and a becoming familiar with the power that does not only found my existence, but constitutes, orders, rules and shapes the living connection of all creaturely existence. At the same time faith is a trust that this power can explicitly relate and does relate to humans, that it expresses a will, that it has a personal form so that we can enter into a living relationship with it.

As soon as we realize the enormous range of this personal power we see that it is adequate to speak of 'faith' in it, since the relationship to it necessarily transcends all knowledge. Yet we must *not oppose* faith and knowledge, since the believing and trusting relationship to God constantly strives for knowledge, for a growing and deepened knowledge and thus is plainly laden with knowledge. A culture and a piety which reduced the relationship to God to *my* relation to an *inner instance* failed to recognize this fact. Over against such destructive reductions we must rediscover the biblical realism which, not only in the so-called 'creation accounts', has its eye on God's creative action in its full range. God links the cosmic forces and the biological forces, the powers of nature and culture. Finally, God includes the humans with the command to dominate vegetation (Genesis 2) and the realm of the animals (Genesis 1).[5]

It is crucial to notice that in the biblical traditions God's creative activity is not simply described as the automatic production of each and every thing, but as an ordered bringing forth, a separating and ruling in which the creatures are given graded participation. If we do not approach the biblical creation accounts superficially and with prejudices of all sorts we can discover that in their simple language full of rich imagery they disclose many truths about the origin and the development of the world. To be sure, they do not have today's cosmological knowledge at their disposal. Above all, they cannot manage large numbers. Historians tell us that the old cultures could obviously not think beyond the number 10,000. But they used powerful images and symbols whose subtlety and depth are often underestimated.

Creation in Just Six Days? The Subtlety of the Biblical Creation Accounts

A typical example of the notorious underestimation of the biblical texts and their knowledge of faith is the widespread opinion that the Bible says God created the world in six times 24 hours ('the work of six days'). Moreover, the creation account is regarded as inconsistent and self-contradictory because it speaks twice of the separation of day and night, once on the first day (Genesis 1.3), and then again after the creation of the sun, the moon and the stars on the fourth day (Genesis 1.14f.). But the seeming naivety reflects on the observers who do not realize that the Bible speaks of *two different time systems*.

On the one hand, it speaks of the 'days of God' and the separation of light and darkness which is not simply the differentiation of natural light and natural darkness. The *days of God* are analogous but different units of time from the *days under the sky*.[6] As already emphasized, the authors of the biblical texts do not have a scientifically exact idea of the extension of these units of time. But they know indeed that for God 'a thousand years are but as yesterday when it is past, or as a watch in the night' (Psalm 90.4). The days of creation thus are very large spaces of time. Within these 'days', cosmic, biological, cultural and religious constellations and processes appear. All these constellations are not self-contained relations. The cosmic constellations, for example, regulate human life on this earth down to the festivals which in their turn are occasions for the encounter with God (Genesis 1.14). Thus the cosmic constellations are perceived in their deep meaning as establishing culture and cult.

Within the days of God, within these large units of time, the evolution of the species of animals and plants occurs which the earth brings forth, and which reproduce and live with each other and from each other (Genesis 1.11ff.). Finally, within these days the creation of humans takes place, who on the one hand are to 'dominate' the world of animals and plants. The language of slave owners expresses the clear dominance of humans over the other creatures. On the other hand, humans, male and female, are to represent the *image of God* for the other creatures. They are thus – in the perception of the Old Testament and the ancient Orient – destined to royal lordship in righteousness and mercy, that is to the exercise of justice and to the protection of the weak.[7]

Thus creation is not at all only the first dark second of the universe, but the whole enormous process from the beginnings of the universe to the creation of humans. Furthermore, creation is the bringing forth not only of nature, but also of culture (with the ruling of the stars and the call to dominion). It is not only creation at the beginning, but also the keeping and ruling of creation (*creatio continua*). Finally, with the climax of the creation in the Sabbath, there is also the setting up of the space for the cultic encounter with God as part of creation. The fact that creation aims at the cult, the encounter of humans with God, and at worship is underscored by the second six-day story (Exodus 24.16) that culminates in the plan for the temple: 'The glory of the Lord settled on Mount Sinai, and the cloud covered it for six days; on the seventh day God called to Moses out of the cloud.'

As early as 1905 Benno Jacob in his book *The Pentateuch* called attention to structural parallels between Genesis 1 and Exodus 24ff.: 'There is no analogy for a period of six days with a following seventh day other than the six workdays with the Sabbath. The six days are the time within which God, hidden in the darkness of the cloud, creates the archetype of the sanctuary in order to call Moses in on the seventh day and to show and explain to him the completed work. This is one of the ... parallels between the six-day creation of the world and the sanctuary.'[8] In recent years, many Jewish and Christian scholars have investigated the interconnection between the creation of the world and the construction of the sanctuary. A deep sense for the analogies between natural, cultural and cultic (liturgical) orders is behind these subtle texts and observations, which calls for further exploration and for growth in our understanding.

Other biblical texts that deal with creation put more emphasis on historical processes in the context of creation. This caused some theologians to claim that creation is mainly concerned with history.[9] However, this playing off against each other of nature and history does not correspond to the biblical understanding of creation. God is the creator – that is the will, the power, the personal instance who creatively connects, orders and shapes nature, culture and history. It is in this complex ordering, governing and ruling that God not only gives the place and space to our lives (and thus also to my life) but above all constitutes the meaning, the direction and the inalienable dignity of human life.

Faith, Witness and the Limits of Naturalistic Thought

With regard to an appreciation of the complexity, the width and the richness of creation, faith always surpasses knowledge. *Faith is a ground for commitment, and a questioning of our commitments; faith includes reliable knowledge, and at the same time it is an awareness of the limits of knowledge.* As faith in the creator it constantly searches for a more comprehensive knowledge of the creator and of creation. But also with regard to the individual existence in creation and its meaning in the context of creation, faith necessarily surpasses knowledge, since *it aims at a fullness and wholeness that discursive knowledge is not able to achieve.* The relationship of my life and our lives to God and to the rest of creation is dynamic and fluent. We see our destination only in fragments. Faith enables us to give this fragmentary perception a specific frame, a trace, a living direction. Faith sees my personal existence, a specific human life, a life-world or a whole historical constellation in the context of God's creation. This specific direction, the authenticity and the specific insight of faith, is lost when the complex and wide view of faith is mistaken for a metaphysic of 'the whole' and when creation is put on a par with all kinds of concepts of totality.

As soon as God's creation is confused with abstract totality, God's names get replaced by terms which seem to honour God but do in fact lose sight of the living God. God is then, for example, called the 'all-determining reality' or the 'all-synthesizing subject' or, even more general, 'the absolute' or 'the ultimate point of reference'. However, faith is clouded in such abstract terms, because the living, formed relationship of the creaturely to God, and God's loving, judging and saving relationship to creation, are lost from view. Some theologians react against this danger by adding to the idea of the abstract whole the thought of an abstract relation of 'the individual' or of 'myself' to God. But again this darkens and empties faith. The problem of the abstract universalization is not eliminated by the addition of the problem of the abstract atomic individualism, but rather heightened. Faith becomes drab, joyless and shapeless. In order to counter these dangers it is helpful to see clearly that faith is not only a personal relationship to God, but also a communal relation to God or the relationship among humans 'before God', as some traditions of the Bible say.

Faith always grows from a community of experience, narration and thought among humans who search for God and love God, who together make an effort to reach a clearer knowledge of God and of God's intentions for the creation. Also in this respect faith always transcends knowledge, provides a frame for knowledge which needs to be disclosed with perseverance. Faith has to live with trust in advance, with the readiness to alter one's own certainty in favour of a greater truth, but also with the readiness to witness, to mediate for others one's own certainty. A characteristic of faith is therefore always that of *witness*, that is of the conviction which at the same time knows that it only grasps part of the reality and truth of which it speaks.[10]

Our description of faith in God the creator – as a living and trusting relationship to the shaping, judging and saving power; to the personal will which keeps together nature, culture and history, and in all this, our lives; and to the personal instance which directs creaturely being and life and gives it its meaning, direction and destination – shows a certain insecurity. 'Power, personal will, personal instance': some people will complain that this certainly needs to be comprehended more clearly. However, Christian faith cannot grasp this instance in a clearer and more definite way without transcending faith in God the creator *alone*. This means that on the one hand faith emphasizes that God's personal relationship to us becomes clear in the fact that God the creator made God's own identity known in Jesus Christ. Faith emphasizes on the other hand that God's power becomes known in the fact that God acts on us and among us in the power of the Holy Spirit. In the power of the Holy Spirit God includes the creatures in the creative activity and even makes them bearers of God's presence on earth.

But for many people this faith in the *Triune God* is still difficult to accept. How can the God who created heaven and earth be revealed and become known in a human, in Jesus of Nazareth? And how can the power and force of the Holy Spirit be brought into a connection with a personal encounter of God and a human being? It is likely that in both cases *naturalistic* limitations of thought and imagination prevent our knowledge of faith from developing further. God the creator is still regarded as the power and the will that is active in nature and at best in a mediated way in culture and history. Contrary to this the biblical texts do not refer to the natural universe alone as 'creation'. When they, for example, speak of 'the heavens', they do not only mean the natural sky from which light, warmth and water come upon the earth. And when they speak of 'the earth', they see it as the place of cultural and historical processes. The earth is not only a natural entity, but also the place of political and social powers and forces, and heaven is also the realm of concrete and specific pasts and futures, the realm withdrawn from our experience from which nevertheless powers and forces act on our lives. Realities unseen, but realities indeed, have to be addressed by faith seeking understanding.[11]

The Holy Spirit is God's creative power through which God directs and rules the fates from heaven and on the earth. The Holy Spirit is the power that brings about righteousness, mercy and the knowledge of God, the power that wakes faith, love and hope. The Holy Spirit is the power in which God's goodness and God's faithfulness among us and in creation can be recognized. This power of the Spirit gains a personal shape in Jesus Christ, who must not only be understood as the pre-Easter historical Jesus, although he makes himself known in him. As the proclaimer of the coming reign of God the pre-Easter Jesus refers to the creative God. As the risen and exalted Christ he mediates the presence of the coming divine reign. He reveals God's creative activity as the bringing forth of the *new creation* among the creatures and in the creation.

With this we stand before a deep secret of faith that poses a severe problem to many people. Why can God not simply reveal the divine identity in creation as we see it? Why does God the creator have to go beyond this identity, so to speak? Why does God take such complicated ways to disclose the creaturely relationship of trust to God? The answer is that creation as nature, as culture and as history *in itself* does not mediate a clear knowledge of God's caring goodness, of God's love and of the destination of humans. Humans fail in their destination to mirror the image of God. They do not adequately give attention to the mandate of dominion. They fail in the search for God and in the love of God. They fail in the fulfilment of God's commandments, and they hinder the realization of God's intentions with the creation. Their image of God becomes correspondingly dark. They look for a wrong kind of support, they make false friends and suffer from unnecessary enmities.

For them God's good creation becomes a threatening and ambivalent environment. Powers detrimental to life take them into their service and enslave them. They look for false help and false helpers. They again pray to the stars and make many kinds of golden calves for themselves. They experiment with numerous gods, ideas and idols that cannot offer any help. But the creator does not respond to this by destroying humans once and for all. God responds with loving mercy. But God's loving mercy does not simply express itself in the fact that God again and again repairs the creation. God's loving mercy expresses itself in the fact that God – even in the midst of judgement and seeming destruction – elevates humans. God's loving mercy expresses itself in God's will for a new creation. It expresses itself in that God rescues creation from the powers of sin and death and gives it a participation in the divine life. The grace and mercy of God comes to us as our ennoblement. This is revealed to humans through Jesus Christ and through the activity of the Spirit. Paradoxical as it may sound, faith in God the creator has to grow beyond itself in order to perceive God's creative power and glory to the fullest.

Comments: Mind and Heart
JOHN POLKINGHORNE

No one writes without some concept of a potential audience in mind. What is written will not be valid for that audience alone, but the shape of the presentation will have been formed, at least to some degree, by the author's notion of who was being addressed. Some of the differences between our pairs of chapters arise from their being oriented towards the interests and concerns of two rather different constituencies (see the Introduction).

In much of my own writing I have in mind either an enquiring member of the scientific community or someone whose approach to religion is influenced both by a consciousness of the intellectual achievements of science and also by a respect for the evidence-based style of thinking so natural to the scientist. In other words, there is often a specific kind of apologetic dimension to what I have to say. By this admission I do not for a moment mean that I seek to adopt a debating-style polemic that tries to exaggerate the positive points and suppress the difficult points in what I have to say. For me, as much as for Michael Welker, the issue of truth is paramount. Christian apologetics can only succeed externally, in helping those enquiring about the faith, if it also succeeds internally by being a careful articulation of Christian experience and understanding, expressed with all the integrity that can be mustered.

It is this kind of apologetic concern, I think, that gives my chapter its rather coolly intellectualist tone when compared with Michael Welker's more passionate writing about 'a living and trusting relationship to the shaping, judging and saving power; to the personal will which keeps together nature, culture and history, and in all this, our lives; and to the personal instance which directs creaturely being and life and gives it its meaning, direction and destination'. The audience that he has had in his writer's eye is, I believe, a church community that is in danger of losing a concern for deep, many-layered theological truth and replacing it with something altogether less profound, focused more on the merely interesting and entertaining than on the rigorous demands of the search for truth about God. I welcome the corrective that Michael's chapter provides to mine, for I fully share his concept of a faith that involves and demands the response of the whole human person to the mystery of the divine Reality. Although I am willing to make an appeal to a kind of natural theology, insightful rather than demonstrative in its status and appealing to the rational beauty and finely tuned fruitfulness of the universe as the grounds for a belief that the cosmos is a creation, I certainly do not suppose that God is simply the ultimate answer to our intellectual curiosity. Although I wish to look through as many windows into reality as possible, I do not believe that our human response is adequately expressed merely by a passive gazing upon that reality.

For this reason, I greatly value Michael Welker's emphasis on the role that the cult should play in our interpretation and understanding of the creation narratives and the doctrine related to them. Here is an intertwining of physical and spiritual experience – one might almost say, anachronistically, of science and religion – in a single thick discourse. A bridge word that both the scientist and the believer will recognize in this regard is 'wonder'.

I consider that our two chapters afford something of a binocular vision onto the great single issue of faith in God the creator. I do so the more readily because I believe that I sense, beneath the differences of our presentations, the presence of a common approach to matters theological, a topic to which we return in Part II.

Reply: 'The Issue of Truth is Paramount'
MICHAEL WELKER

I wholeheartedly agree that 'the issue of truth is paramount' for both of us. I indeed write for a church community that, as John Polkinghorne says, is 'in danger of losing a concern for deep, many-layered theological truth'. I see two threats against which I try to work. One threat is that theological symbols and contents become regarded as a resource for cultural manipulation, without any consideration for their inner consistencies and rationalities. Pick this image, mix it with that story, do what you want to do, as long as it is entertaining or provocative! This increasing mentality in our classic main-line churches is devastating. It destroys faith and it destroys the *churches from the inside. I think that the two of us would like to encourage and even challenge both pious people and educated lay people, even the despisers of Christian faith, to take the language and the subject matters of faith seriously. It is understandable that persons with a more emotional or moral interest want this 'nice' theology and theologians, warm and entertaining, empathetic and therapeutically oriented. I think that the concern for truth must not be exchanged for these gifts, even if seen as gifts of the Spirit.*

Then there is a second threat. This is a theological reductionism, often connected with an intellectual minimalism, which reduces the basic contents of faith to highly secularized and even distortive thoughts and ideas. This reductionism can be found among philosophically and culturally trained and interested people, even in the academy. Very often it offers itself as the solution in dialogue between religion and secularity or in dialogue between different religions. The formula could run like this: Let's at least agree on God as 'the all-synthesizing subject' or on the fact that 'everybody has an inner relation to a transcendent other in his or her inner self'. These are such reductionistic ideas which can destroy the serious search for truth. After my thorough studies of several great philosophies I am very suspicious of such paradigmatic minimalism. The 'simple' ideas become all too often misleading abstractions, or even intellectual and religious traps, which are hard to escape.

Certainly, we cannot avoid reductions and abstractions. But also in the realm of theology we should follow Whitehead's advice: 'Seek simplicity – and distrust it!' I see both of us challenging our contemporaries to engage in a critical and self-critical realism which takes the contents of faith and the historical, cultural, canonical and theological weight of the biblical traditions seriously. In the second part of this book we shall address these issues more extensively.

NOTES

1. Cf. M. Welker, '"Whoever Does Not Love Abides in Death" (1 John 3.14b): Romantic Love, Covenantal Love, Kenotic Love', in John Polkinghorne (ed.), *Love as the Ultimate Nature of Reality*, Eerdmans and SPCK, 2001.
2. Martin Luther, *The Small Catechism* (1529), *Creeds of the Churches: A Reader in Christian Doctrine from the Bible to the Present*, 3rd edn, ed. John H. Leith, John Knox, 1982, p. 115.

3. Luther, *Small Catechism*, p. 115 (the very free translation has been corrected in comparison with the German original, M.W.)

4. *Luther's Large Catechism*, Anniversary Translation, Luther Publishing House, 1983, p. 111.

5. For the details of these rich accounts see, M. Welker, *Creation and Reality: Theological and Biblical Perspectives*, Warfield Lectures 1991, Fortress Press, 1999; Karl Löning and Erich Zenger, Als Anfang schuf Gott: Biblische Schöpfungstheologien, Patmos, 1997.

6. Odil Hannes Steck, *Der Schöpfungsbericht der Priesterschrift: Studien zur literarkritischen und überlieferungsgeschichtlichen Problematik von Genesis 1.1–2, 4a*, rev. edn, Vandenhoeck, 1981, pp. 112–13 and 161ff.; M. Welker, 'Creation: Big Bang or the Work of Seven Days?' *Theology Today* 52 (1995), pp. 173–87.

7. Cf. *Creation and Reality*, ch. 5: 'Creation, the Image of God, and the Mandate of Dominion'.

8. *Der Pentateuch: Exegetisch-kritische Forschungen*, von Veit & Comp., 1905, pp. 157–8 (translation M.W.).

9. For example Karl Barth, *Church Dogmatics*, III/1.

10. Hans-Georg Gadamer first drew my attention to this texture of the 'witness'.

11. John Polkinghorne and Michael Welker, Introduction to *The End of the World and the Ends of God: Science and Theology on Eschatology*, Trinity Press, 2000, pp. 1–13. See also Part II of this book.

3

FAITH IN CHRIST

JOHN POLKINGHORNE

Beyond Deism

In my first chapter I suggested that the rational and beautifully ordered structure of the universe was supportive of the idea that the divine mind lay behind its being, and that the fruitful process of cosmic evolution, realizing an anthropic potentiality with which the world was already endowed, was similarly supportive of the idea that the purposes of God lay behind the universe's unfolding history. If these arguments were to be granted their maximum force, they would still only lead to the idea of God as the Great Mathematician or the Architect of the Universe. On its own, this concept need correspond to no more than the God of deism, with so little to do that fading away into nothingness is the perpetual risk of so minimal a deity. To these ideas I added that of God as the ground of value, a move that began to turn the argument in a direction in which the use of personal language for the divine (of course, employed in a 'stretched' or analogical sense) begins to become appropriate. Finally, considering ultimate cosmic and human futility led to the bold move of asserting that God will also be found to be the God who is the ground of hope in a destiny beyond death.

Immediately, a quizzical and enquiring friend might ask what is the basis for making this last claim. Is it, in fact, no more than an attempt at whistling in the dark to keep our spirits up? We are faced with the fundamental question that exercised the young Luther so much, Is God gracious towards humanity? Does the deity care for individual human beings? Can God be trusted? None of the windows through which we have peered so far will give us access to the answers to these questions. That is even true of the window we labelled 'religious experience', for we did not see through it on that occasion more than a general, and somewhat confused, picture of encounter with the sacred. So specific an issue as the one we are now considering can only be addressed in correspondingly specific terms. To have any chance of making progress we have to be willing to move from general arguments to the consideration of the claims of a more specific kind of revelation, understood, as we discussed before, as involving particular events and particular persons believed to afford particularly transparent access to encounter with the divine.

Personal Engagement

It is necessary to recognize at once that there is an epistemic problem. The significance of these events and these persons is not a matter that can be assessed impartially by a wholly detached observer. As in the familiar case of the estimation of individual human character, some personal engagement is indispensable. A detached observer might interpret Jack's expensive gift to Joan as an act of generosity or as an act of ostentatious extravagance, and only closer encounter will settle the issue. An unengaged spectator of the exit of Israel from Egypt would have seen only the fortunate coincidence that a strong wind drove back the waters of the Reed Sea, allowing the fleeing slaves to get across before the wind dropped again and the waters returned to engulf their Egyptian pursuers. That this was God's great act of delivering Israel from bondage, a redemptive deed that would be of constitutive and continuing significance, could only be known, were it to be known at all, from within the company of the faithful.

The discipline of religious studies has a valuable concern to record the phenomena of religious traditions, but the true theological character of these traditions can only be known from within each one. This necessary commitment to a point of view does not imply that the insights thus derived are simply tricks of the perspective adopted. Science itself begins, and mere natural history ends, when we begin to survey the physical world from a chosen interpretative point of view. Hence the inescapable intertwining of theory and experiment in science, with scientists wearing, as Russell Hanson once said, 'spectacles behind the eyes'. In both science and theology, interpretation and experience intertwine to form the hermeneutic circle: the attainment of understanding requires a corrigible commitment to initial belief; belief is sustained by the understanding that it affords.

In the realm of the personal and the transpersonal, the degree of commitment involved is very much greater than in science, for it goes far beyond adherence to a selected cognitive point of view, embracing, as it does, the set of a total way of life. I cannot know you as my friend unless I am willing to accept the obligations of trust and mutuality that friendship implies. Because of the ambiguities and uncertainties inherent in any human meeting, there is an unavoidable element of risk involved. To an even greater degree, we cannot know God just as the basis of a 'Theory of Everything' that satisfies our intellectual curiosity. Awe and worship and obedience are indispensable elements in any true encounter with the divine. Thus, although religious faith certainly involves appeal to motivated belief, it goes beyond cool, rational discernment to require the response of the heart and will, as well as the assent of the mind.

While science involves this adoption of a prior perspective, we must also acknowledge that the correction of that point of view (revision of the formula for the lenses in those spectacles behind the eyes) is much more readily effected in science than may appear to be the case within the religious traditions. The nudges of nature, the unexpected experimental findings that challenge current orthodoxy, are often resisted by the scientific leaders of the day, but in the end empirical adequacy is an indispensable component in the successful attainment of scientific understanding. In the end, the dust settles and questions get answered to universal satisfaction in a way that is very impressive. Religious traditions, on the other hand, not only exhibit a perplexing degree of dissonance between themselves, but within each tradition they may also appear to display a great stability of doctrine – though anyone with an acquaintance with the history of theological thinking will be aware that stability is not the same thing as unchanging rigidity. There is development of doctrine, even if it is confined within the limits of a degree of orthodox consonance with the foundational experiences and insights of the tradition. This trajectory of consonance is vital, for religious communities cannot maintain an authentic identity without preserving a due respect for their defining origins. The empirical (better, experiential) adequacy that theology requires cannot be contained within a single generation, but it stretches over time.

No one acquainted with the practice of science could be unaware of the important role that the community of scientists plays in the enterprise of discovery. Without granting that community an infallible status, its sifting and eventual acceptance of new proposals has been an important feature of scientific progress. The community's ability to reach conclusions that in due course are universally accepted is very striking. In a religious tradition, the community of the faithful also has an important role to play, not least in resolving the ambiguities and dangers inherent in individual experience and idiosyncratic interpretation. Religion is always peculiarly open to the possibility of distortion and deception. Hence the recognized need for spiritual direction and the care with which spiritual directors seek to sift the authentic from the spurious, or even the demonic. Protestant emphasis on the religious response of the individual needs a counterpoise in the Catholic and Orthodox emphasis on respect for the tradition and for the judgement of the whole Church in matters of the reception of new theological insights. Once again, for theology the relevant truth-seeking community cannot be restricted to the contemporary. Religious understanding is not cumulative in the way that scientific understanding is, so that there is no presumptive superiority of the insight of the present over that of the past. The company of witnesses whose testimony is to be heeded is spread over many generations.

With these considerations in mind, it is clear that the answers to the questions posed at the beginning of this chapter have to be pursued within a chosen tradition and they cannot be addressed in a detached and unearthed manner. The choice I make is that of an avowedly Christian understanding, for this is what undergirds my own spiritual experience and correlates with my understanding of reality. This acceptance of particularity accords with the rational strategy of seeking to conform the search for knowledge to the nature of the subject about which knowledge is sought. There is no neutral point from which we may assess the God of Israel and the Father of our Lord Jesus Christ. It is claimed (and I believe) that this God has revealed the divine nature in specific historical contexts and it is only by engaging with these particularities that we shall be able to pursue the issue of faith in that God. Accordingly, I now turn to the specific consideration of faith in Christ.[1]

Jesus of Nazareth

For the Christian, the focus of attention is Jesus of Nazareth. At once, our 'window' metaphor is shattered, to be replaced by encounter with a person. For Christianity, God's word is not primarily a written revelation, but it has been uttered in the life of Jesus. The Bible does not derive its authority from being a divinely dictated text (as Muslims believe the Qur'an to be), but as the record of God's dealings with Israel, eventually culminating in this first-century Jew, whose life, death and resurrection are then recounted, together with the early history of his followers. The personal is the relational, so that in revelation in Christ there must be a transactional exchange both from the side of divinity and from the side of humanity. What this could mean, and why one might believe it to be so, are matters still to be addressed. Such a discussion cannot even begin, however, unless one is willing to contemplate the possibility of such an amazing 'scandal of particularity'.

It is easy to recognize that from time to time there are persons of genius and profound insight who deeply affect the experience and understanding of the generations that follow them. The scientific role of honour – Galileo, Newton, Darwin, Einstein . . . – makes the point clearly enough. In the more personal realm of, say, the aesthetic, one can see that such great figures are unique and irreplaceable. Only Beethoven could have composed the late quartets. The founding figures of the great faith traditions – Moses, Buddha, Muhammad – can be fitted into such a scheme, relating to the way in which they were inspired to offer new insight into the nature of the sacred. If we consider Jesus simply as a great teacher, a charismatic leader, a fearless prophet, then he too finds a place under that rubric. But that is precisely *not* how his followers down the ages, from the first disciples and on to the successive generations of the Church, have categorized him. Instead, they have used altogether more radical and startling categories. Acts portrays Peter as standing up in Jerusalem a few weeks after the crucifixion and proclaiming that Jesus is God's 'Lord and Anointed One', the person through whom human beings are to receive forgiveness of their sins, the one who has been exalted to the right hand of God. In his first epistle to the Thessalonians (probably the earliest Christian writing we possess) Paul speaks of Jesus using the divine title 'Lord' and asserting that it is through him that we shall all find salvation (5.9) and will be restored again to life after death (4.14). A remarkable degree of intimacy is being claimed to exist between the one God of Israel and the crucified and exalted Jesus Christ.

Can one really attach such significance to a wandering preacher and wonder-worker who lived long ago in a peripheral province of the Roman Empire? It is important to recognize that the mainstream of Christian thinking, while making huge claims for the universal significance of Jesus, has not sought to avoid the scandal of his particularity. For the Church at its most faithful, Jesus has always been a first-century Jew (whatever more there might also be to say), and not a timeless Universal Man, nor a docetic Heavenly Figure, only appearing to be in human form.

If we were right to think that the coming to be of persons was a highly significant event in cosmic history, then the category of the personal is one we may expect to be of corresponding importance in our understanding of reality. If that reality has its origin in the will of a transpersonal God, then we may expect the personal, in all its necessary particularity, to be the prime vehicle for the creator's revelatory interaction with creation. At least, the possibility that the revealing of the divine nature and the fulfilment of the divine will has been most precisely focused in a single person is surely something that is worth investigating. It is the character of the personal that it is expressed in the unique. To refuse the scandal of particularity would be to decline the significance of the personal.

Our sources for the origin of beliefs about Jesus, and the prime evidence on which such beliefs might be based, are the writings of the New Testament. No body of literature has been subject to such unending study, or been the subject of so many and varied assessments. The arguments that follow are, I believe, derivable with some care from such a study, but the actual defence of that proposition cannot be set out in any detail here.[2]

The first thing that strikes one about the story of Jesus is how markedly it differs from those of other great founders of religious traditions. Moses, the Buddha, Muhammad, all die in honoured old age, surrounded by their faithful followers who are resolved to carry on the work and message of the master. Jesus dies in mid-life, deserted by his followers, subjected to a painful and shameful death, and with the cry 'My God, my God, why have you forsaken me?' on his lips (Mark 15.43; Matthew 27.46). On the face of it, it looks like total defeat. The story of Jesus is a highly ambiguous story. If it ends at Calvary, it portrays someone who, at best, met death with just a little less fortitude than many other martyrs, and certainly without the serenity of Socrates. At worst, it closed with the final disillusionment of a deluded man. If that was what was going on, and if the story of Jesus ended there, I think that we would never have heard of him. He would just have disappeared from history, as many other defeated or mistaken people must have done. That we have heard of him is, therefore, very significant. From the first, his followers have claimed that God resolved the ambiguity and that the story of Jesus continued in his risen and glorified life, the other side of death.

The Resurrection

The resurrection is the pivot on which faith in Christ turns. This is not the place to attempt a detailed evaluation of the evidence and motivation for such a belief, nor a discussion of what the character of such an event could have been, with both its transhistorical significance and also its claimed deposit within history. These are tasks that I have attempted elsewhere.[3] It is important that such a discussion is possible, that belief in the resurrection is not an ungrounded assertion, independent of any engagement with historical evidence. Neither is the assessment of the weight of that evidence independent of the degree of meaning we can give to the claim that Jesus was more than a wandering prophet. Here, as always, there is no escape from the hermeneutic circle, in which experience and interpretation inextricably intertwine, just as theory and experiment do in science.

The resurrection of Jesus has its own scandal of particularity, for it is only of this man that it is claimed that, within history, he has been raised to a new, glorified and everlasting life beyond history. If that is true, there must be something unique, and uniquely significant, about Jesus. I believe that it is true and that any adequate account of faith in Christ must rest on its truth. It is on that basis that I continue the discussion of what the uniqueness of Jesus might be. (It is my belief that the rational need to make sense of the phenomenon of Jesus Christ will force us to conclusions as initially strange and counterintuitive as those forced upon the pioneers of quantum theory in their encounter with the subatomic physical world.)

As one reads the New Testament, one has a strong impression that the writers, in all the diversity of viewpoint and expression that they exhibit, have nevertheless an important experience in common. They are all wrestling with the attempt to give an adequate account of their encounter with Christ, their risen Lord, and what he means to them in their lives.[4] At the heart of this struggle are two paradoxes, neither to be denied nor easily understood. One is that of the crucified messiah. They believe that Jesus is God's chosen and anointed one, but he has proved to be no Davidic king bringing military deliverance, and the salvation he brought (forgiveness of sins and a new transforming life) is intimately connected with his painful and shameful death. The second paradox is less clearly focused but even more remarkable. The New Testament writers believe that after his resurrection, Jesus has been exalted to 'the right hand of God' (the position of authority and power). They assign to him the title 'Lord', despite the fact that they know that this really belongs to the one God of Israel. They even apply to him texts from the prophets that clearly speak in the original of Israel's God. Paul expresses the initial greeting in most of his letters by using the curious juxtaposition, 'God our Father and the Lord Jesus Christ', an extraordinary association for a pious first-century Jew to make. In short, the writers seem driven to use divine as well as human language about Jesus, without giving up their Jewish monotheism. Within the New Testament itself, these tensions are unresolved, but clearly the situation was intellectually unstable and it had to become, as it did in the subsequent history of the Church, the subject of much more theological argument and attempted resolution.

A scientist, and particularly one who has worked in fundamental physics, will not find the situation altogether unfamiliar.[5] There are times in the history of science – the period 1900–26, in which quantum theory came to birth, would be one of them – in which strange and perplexing experience heralds a radical revision of previously cherished beliefs. For a while all is confusion and threatened paradox: light shows wave-like behaviour; light shows particle-like behaviour. Initially all that can be done is to hold fast to experience by the skin of one's intellectual teeth, resisting the temptation to return to the simple life by neglecting part of the apparently conflicting evidence. People have to cling to the belief that nature will be found to be rational in its behaviour, if only one can construe that rationality in the appropriate way. In the case of quantum theory, this intellectual fortitude was rewarded by the eventual discovery of a theory that allowed very successful explanations of phenomena, even if the deeper attainment of complete understanding still eludes us, because of a lack of agreement and success in deciding in detail how the formalism is to be interpreted in direct physical terms. In the case of the Church's centuries of engagement with the problem of how to articulate an adequate understanding of the implications of faith in Christ, the results have been less extensive. (Theology is more difficult than physics.) The famous Chalcedonian Definition of 451 does little more than indicate the area of discourse within which understanding must be sought if it is to be adequate to foundational and continuing Christian experience. In effect, it asserts that an adequate expression of the insights of the Church requires that both human language and divine language have to be used about Jesus Christ, without any attempt to assimilate one language to the other. The Council did not settle the detailed form that this discourse must take, and many centuries of further effort have not completed the task.

Christian Belief

Scientists instinctively respond to profound ideas that bring unexpected illumination to previously dark and difficult areas. They are also aware that such ideas are often very surprising and may well initially seem counterintuitive. Orthodox Christian faith in Christ is based on two profound and illuminating ideas, each mysterious and challenging in its character and exciting in its implications.

(1) *Incarnation*. The New Testament writers were driven to use both human and divine language about Jesus precisely because in his life there is both the life of humanity and the life of God. 'God was in Christ' (2 Corinthians 5.19); 'He reflects the glory of God and bears the very stamp of his nature, upholding the universe by his word of power' (Hebrews 1.3); 'In the beginning was the Word ... and the Word was God ... and the Word became flesh and dwelt among us' (John 1.1 and 14). This happened without the obliteration of the human. The infinite and eternal became focused on the finite and the temporal. God was made known to humanity in the plainest possible terms by living the life of a man. If we want to know if God is gracious to us, we look to see how Jesus treated those he met in the course of his earthly life and how he spoke about his heavenly Father. Obviously there are many difficulties about the coherence and intelligibility of such an amazing idea. The divine governance of the universe could not have been interrupted, as if the throne of the universe had been empty during the period of Jesus' life in Palestine. Eventually this led to an understanding in terms of the doctrine of the Trinity and the incarnation of the second Person. While intellectual integrity requires the Christian theological community to continue to struggle with these deep issues, faith in Christ does not depend upon their totally successful resolution. This is because the basis of that faith lies in experience, the continuing Christian experience that

in Jesus we encounter our own humanity (he is one of us) but also the life of God (the One who is thus discovered to be gracious to us). No scientist could rejoice in ignorance or lack of understanding, but all scientists know the primacy of the way things are found to be over our difficulties in comprehending how it comes about that things are this way.

(2) *The crucified God.* The incarnation was not just a divine sharing in human life so that we might have a better comprehension of the divine life and nature. It was also that God might, fully and to the uttermost, participate in the creaturely life of humanity, even to the point of the desolation and death on the cross. Jürgen Moltmann has taught us that the Christian God is the crucified God.[6] Here we encounter a unique and profound Christian response to the problem of suffering. God is not just a compassionate spectator of the strange and often bitter history of creation. The Christian God has been a participant within that pilgrimage of pain, so that in Christ we truly see the divine 'fellow sufferer who understands'. The insight meets the problems of theodicy at the deep level that they demand. It does not dispel all our perplexities, but it confronts and accepts these difficulties in a way commensurate with their profundity. For Christian believers, troubled as we are by the problem of evil, belief in God is made possible by faith in Christ, the incarnate One who in Gethsemane and on the cross shared the human lot, even to the point of accepting reluctance at the approach of death and the experience of desolation that comes from a feeling of Godforsakenness. Yet that sharing was not simply a divine solidarity in creaturely victimization, for the resurrection, and its aftermath in the life of the Christian community, revealed that Christ's sacrificial death on Calvary is the origin and ground of human reconciliation with God, and the hope of a destiny beyond death in the everlasting life of God's new creation.

It is important to recognize that these two great Christian concepts only carry the force that has been attributed to them if they really refer to events that have actually taken place and to a God who was truly present in Jesus Christ as more than simply being the source of his spiritual inspiration. The idea of God's participation in creaturely life, even to the paradoxical point of a divine assumption of suffering and death, is a very powerful story, but if it were no more than a symbolic tale, in the end it would leave us only with the pathos of the wistful feeling, 'Would that it actually had been so'. The Christian story produces faith in Christ precisely as it is seen to have been an *enacted* story, combining the force of metaphorical symbol (our least inadequate human resource for speaking of the mystery of God) with the force of actual historical happening (the unique impact of a true story).

> The power of myth and the power of actuality fuse in the incarnation. What could be more profound than that God should take human form, make himself known in human terms, sharing the suffering of the strange world he has made and on the cross open his arms to embrace its bitterness? That is a story that moves me at the deepest level. Yet it is no tale projected on a shadowy figure of ancient legend. It is concerned with what actually happened in the concrete person of Jesus Christ, a wandering preacher in a peripheral province of the Roman empire, at a particular point in history. The centre of Christianity lies in the *realised myth* of the incarnation.[7]

Although Christian belief must appeal to the foundational events of the past, that appeal will lose its power if it is not also found to correspond in some consonant way to the experience of the present. I have already spoken of the company of witnesses spread out through time. The resurrection appearances and the finding of the empty tomb are located in the first century, but in every century the Church has spoken of Jesus Christ as its living Lord in the present. It does not simply look back to a revered founder figure of the past but, particularly in its experience of the presence of Christ in the action of the gathered eucharistic community, obeying the Lord's command to do this in remembrance of him, it believes it bears witness to the One who is ever contemporary. Of course, those who stand outside the Church may feel reserve about this testimony, but it is part of the motivating evidence for faith in Christ. We are back again with the point of the necessity of seeking knowledge of God from within the tradition and experience of a faith community.

This experience resonates with the claim, made so clearly in the New Testament, that there is new life to be found through faith in the risen Lord. It is to these issues of soteriology, of the benefits that Christ brings to those who trust in him and receive him, that I must now turn. Faith in Christ is concerned not only with access to knowledge but with the transformation of the whole of life, for it involves the response of the emotions and the will as well as the mind. This transforming power both derives from who Christ is and it also bears witness to who he is. There is no need for us to choose between an objective Christology (Christ's intrinsic nature) and a subjective Christology (Christ in my experience), for they are complementary aspects of our encounter with the single reality of the incarnation. If I am to know Jesus truly, it can only be as my Lord; if I confess him as my Lord, that is because that is who he really is.

It is the manifest conviction of the New Testament writers that the life and death and resurrection of Jesus Christ have brought about new possibilities for human life which, while they had been in the eternal purposes of God, had not previously been fully realized within created history. These new possibilities centre on two themes that are complementary to each other: deliverance from the bondage of sin, and entry into the life of the new creation that has been inaugurated by Christ's resurrection.

In our earlier consideration of created reality we recognized the (empirically verifiable) fact of the moral distortion of human life that Christian theology calls 'sin' and attributes to an alienation of humanity from God. Jesus Christ, true God and true man, is the ontological point of meeting between the divine life and the life of creation. Here then is the bridge by which the two may be rejoined and the alienation removed 'in Christ'. That moral distortion of life that is sin, and the deposit of spiritual malformation resulting from chosen deeds of evil and rebellion, that are sins, can have their remedy. Forgiveness is made available by which even the past may be healed and broken relationships restored, both individually and communally. Such a great act of redemptive transformation is not costless, as if it were an effortless exercise of divine power by a God who is fundamentally immune from the impact of creaturely sinfulness, or fundamentally indifferent to the immoral doings of puny creatures. We know from our interpersonal human experiences that truly to recognize an injury done, and then truly to forgive that injury, is a costly matter, both for the one forgiving and for the one forgiven. It is far removed from a trivial politeness that says, 'It doesn't really matter. Forget it.'

Faith in Christ sees Jesus' death on the cross as being the cost of our forgiveness. 'Christ died for our sins in accordance with the scriptures' (1 Corinthians 15.3). Nowhere is the difference between experience and the understanding of that experience more clearly exemplified theologically than in Christian thinking about this fact of the atonement. That in

Christ we are delivered from the thrall of the past, and from the bondage of sin, has been Christian testimony from the beginning. That this power of divine forgiveness originates in, and is revealed by, the painful and shameful sacrificial event of the crucifixion has been equally clearly affirmed. Yet how this comes about has been as variously explored, and with as little agreed total success, as has been the case with the quantum theorists' attempts to understand the nature of the measurement process. Obviously, measurements are made on quantum systems; obviously (at least, it is obvious within the Christian community) we are forgiven our sins through the death of Christ. How these things happen we do not know. This is not the place to review so-called theories of the atonement,[8] though we shall be delivered from morally unsatisfactory accounts of the propitiation of an angry God if we heed Moltmann's insight to understand Calvary as a Trinitarian event, involving the costly participation of Father, Son and Holy Spirit. The *fact* of the atonement, however, is of central importance for faith in Christ.

Equally central is the conviction that 'if anyone is in Christ, he is a new creation; the old has passed away, behold, the new has come' (2 Corinthians 5.17). The resurrection of Jesus is seen as the seminal event from which a new creative work of God has begun to grow. This new creation does not involve the abolition of the old creation, but rather its redemptive transformation. It is a creation *ex vetere*, out of the old, and not a second creation *ex nihilo*.[9] That is why the tomb was empty. The Lord's risen body is the transfigured and glorified form of his dead body. This eschatological transformation of the matter of the corpse of Jesus signifies that in Christ there is a destiny for the whole material creation, and not just for humankind alone (Colossians 1.20).

Human beings and the whole created order (Romans 8.19–21) will participate fully in this new creation in the eschatological future that lies beyond our deaths and the death of the whole universe. The credibility of Christian faith and hope depends upon a belief that the ultimate word about the significance of life lies with God and not with death.[10] However, in accordance with the tension between the 'not yet' and the 'already', always encountered in Christian thinking about eschatology, faith in Christ will also involve a foretaste of eternal life within the transience of this world of mortality. This is the positive experience of new life in Christ that accompanies the consciousness of sins forgiven and divine grace bestowed.

So brief a soteriological summary is in danger of presenting too dichotomous an account, as if cross and forgiveness, resurrection and new life, were separable entities. In fact, they belong inseparably together in the single experience of faith in Christ. In the liturgy, and so in all great musical settings of the Mass, the solemnity of the *crucifixus est* is followed immediately by the joyfulness of the *et resurrexit*. But how are we to understand this single work of Christ? How does the death of this one man avail for all humanity? How does his victory over death avail for all other mortals? Of course, the incarnation implies that God is also a party to these events within creation, but how are we human beings, living centuries later, also to be a party to them, so that we too share in their salvific fruitfulness?

I do not think that we shall make much headway with this critical issue unless we are prepared to look afresh at the notion of autonomous individuality that is so basic an assumption in our atomized Western culture. In the eighteenth century physicists saw space as a container within which individual atoms were in motion and occasional collision. For many reasons, including relativity and chaos theory, we have come to revise that physical picture. Space–time–matter constitute an inseparable 'package deal', according to Einsten's general theory of relativity. Chaotic systems are too sensitive to their circumstances ever to be isolatable from the effects of their environment, and complex systems manifest holistic pattern-forming powers that one would never guess simply from thinking about their individual components. Above all, quantum theory's discovery of the so-called 'EPR effect' shows that even the subatomic world cannot be treated atomistically, but it possesses an intrinsic degree of 'togetherness-in-separation'.[11] Once two quantum entities have interacted with each other, they retain a counterintuitive power of instantaneous influence upon each other, however widely they separate. They cannot escape from mutual entanglement.

If these patterns of interrelationality are present in the physical world, would it not be reasonable to expect there to be their counterparts in the realm of the personal? Hints to this effect come to us from non-Western societies. Tribal cultures in Africa and elsewhere retain a strong sense and experience of the communal. There is some degree of sub-oceanic linkage of the ego islands of single human beings.[12]

Faith in Christ is not merely concerned with the beliefs, decisions and actions of individuals, important as they must be acknowledged to be. There is also a corporate dimension, most clearly expressed in the Pauline doctrine of the body of Christ (Romans 12; 1 Corinthians 12;

Ephesians 4). Although Christ is unquestionably identified with the crucified and exalted individual who was Jesus of Nazareth, the New Testament writers also found a need to speak of the reality of Christ in inclusive and communal terms, proclaiming a solidarity with him into which believers are incorporated *en Christo*.[13] Mysterious and difficult as these ideas are for us today, I think that it is along these lines that we shall be able to understand more fully the salvific effectiveness of Christ 'for us'.

Faith in Christ is mysterious, challenging, exciting, rooted in Christian experience, both original and contemporary. It goes far beyond the inspiration one might draw from a striking individual or a remarkable story. First and foremost, it is concerned with the good news about how God is gracious to us and how our reconciliation with our creator will afford us the power of new life, without which the *imitatio Christi*, the resolve to follow the pattern of Jesus' selfless life, would be no more than a frustrating impossibility. This good news is not presented to us for our information but for our response and committed acceptance. Faith in Christ is grounded in the enacted events of history and, despite Lessing's well known protest that such contingent facts could never be the ground of the necessary truths of reason, the story of Jesus gives us insights into God and God's ways that are of everlasting significance. It has about it all the surprise and profound insight that one might expect of a deep understanding of reality. It has all the challenge and hope of a radically transforming power of life. It is the basis of entering into all that is true about humanity as God intends us to be.

Comments: Critical and Self-Critical Realism

MICHAEL WELKER

I find the description of the analogies and the differences between 'faith seeking understanding' and 'science seeking understanding' very illuminating. It helps us to see why it is so important to deal with central theological topics in canonic and ecumenical spectra of perspectives. It helps us to see why the mere attempt to grasp the contents of faith within the boundaries of one philosophy or one Zeitgeist will run into problems and dissatisfaction. But the canonic traditions of the Bible include more than a thousand years of spiritual experience. They present us with a 'pluralistic library' (Heinz

Schürmann) that offers different Sitze im Leben *(settings in life) with different, often complementary and sometimes conflicting perspectives on God and God's intentions with creation. To give just one rough example: Human beings will ask in one way for God's rescue when they suffer from tyranny, and in another way when they suffer from chaos.*

It is crucial that theology and faith do not try to smooth away these tensions. They challenge our 'realism'. Of course, we cannot escape our common sense, our morals, our cultural settings. But we can become open for their transformation. In my opinion the critical and self-critical realism that we share is such a dynamic realism.

You challenge us to regard the incarnation as God's invitation to encounter the glory of God in a way that is attuned to our finite life and frail experience. And this not only on a cognitive level, but certainly not without it. You emphasize the richness of God's revelation in Christ without forgetting to address the problem of the particularity of his earthly life. Through this revelation God does not only mediate to us insight and understanding of the divine plans for creation. God also provides us with many ways of freeing us from bondage, of opening our lives to God's purposes and of enabling us to become witnesses and even bearers of the divine life in the midst of creation.

Let me add three observations to your Christological contribution.

What does the cross reveal?

Luther, Hegel, Bonhoeffer, Moltmann and other theologians have power-fully emphasized that the cross of Christ reveals the suffering God, even 'the crucified God'. You have quoted Whitehead's recommendation that we should not understand God 'in the image of an imperial ruler, ... of a personification of moral energy, ... of an ultimate philosophical principle', but as 'the fellow sufferer who understands'. But I think that the cross also reveals the 'sin of the world' in the conspiracy of religion, politics, law (both Roman and Jewish), of public opinion and moral sense against the presence of God. It thus awakens expectations of a transforming restitution of the principalities and powers that have such an impact on our lives. The 'law of the Spirit', the 'law of Christ', the 'law of faith' replaces the law which has fallen under the dominion of sin. This restitution, it seems to me, is not just effected by substituting the 'suffering' for the 'dominating' God. The cross moves beyond that opposition.

It was the Princeton Old Testament scholar Patrick Miller who first sensitized me to this. In a discussion of Isaiah 42.2 ('He will not cry or lift up his voice, or make it heard in the street') – a text explicitly applied to Jesus by Matthew 12.18ff. – he stated that at least two of the three expressions used by Isaiah for the 'cry in the street' refer to the 'cry of a victim'. So we cannot simply oppose the cry of the suffering victim to the shouting of the imperial ruler. We have to transcend the alternative: acquiring loyalty 'from above' or 'from below'. The 'messianic secret', the emergent working of the resurrection witnesses, the emergent 'coming of God's reign' and the pouring of the Spirit point to this alternative beyond the dualities like ruling or suffering, dominion or resistance: the transformation of the principalities and powers whose corruptedness and helplessness is revealed by the cross does not come in a monohierarchical way. It comes from many sources and many sides.

The fullness of Christ's life in the resurrection

This polyphony is compatible with the 'personal' presence of Christ that you underscore in your contribution. The personal presence of the resurrected includes the fullness of his pre-Easterly life, with its many dimensions. This life offers many spaces for discipleship and witness. From Jesus' turning to the children and to sick, suffering, possessed persons through his 'symbol-political conflicts' (Gerd Theissen) with Rome and Jerusalem to his reinterpretation of the Old Testament law, numerous connections are imaginable which shape certain images of Jesus and styles of piety. The working of the Spirit and the constitution of faith come with a richness of religious forms although they are all concentrated on the incarnate, crucified, resurrected and coming Christ.

As you point out, the holy communion gives us a rich, yet clear perspective on this orientation. In the communion the whole Christ is present: the pre-Easter Jesus whom we remember, the crucified One whom we proclaim, the risen One to whom we bear witness, and the human One whom we expect and await. In the celebration of the Supper, the gathered community is permeated and surrounded by Christ, by the entire richness of his life. The Reformers preferred to speak of Christ's 'real presence' instead of his 'personal presence'. It seems to me worthy of further discussion, whether the term 'real presence' is better suited than that of Christ's 'personal presence' to provide a framework for the difficult task of understanding this complex of relations, or whether we will even have to move beyond this alternative.

Sacrifice and victimization

You rightly insist that we cannot give up the talk about 'sacrifice' and 'atonement' in connection with the cross of Christ. In what way do we have to understand Jesus Christ's offering 'himself as a sacrifice'? In a pioneer work, Sigrid Brandt has continued and advanced the theological path proceeding from the insights into 'atonement' won by Gese, Janowski and other biblical scholars.[14] She highlights a distinction that German and some other languages, unlike English, unfortunately do not make. The German word Opfer *can be translated into English as both 'sacrifice' and 'victim'. This problem of some languages is connected with a problem in substance, since many sacrifices claim to need a victim. But not every sacrifice is necessarily tied to victimization. And by no means is it permissible to religiously cloud the issue of victimization by terming victims 'sacrifices'. Many instances of victimization attempt deceitfully to consecrate the destruction or killing of human beings by using the language of 'sacrifice'. (The victims of war must be 'offered' so that the people can live; the many traffic victims must be 'sacrificed' to the advantage of automobile culture and individual transportation, etc.)*

In precisely this sense, Jesus' victimization on the cross can be masked by saying that God willed. that Jesus be victimized. In opposition to such pernicious masking strategies, Brandt shows that the incarnation of Jesus Christ is already a sacrifice: in the incarnation, God 'gives' God's self to the world of human beings. The divine life becomes subject to confusion with earthly life; the divine life becomes vulnerable. In this sense, the divine life is 'given' as a sacrifice. But this does not mean that God willed – or even planned and intended! – the victimization of Jesus on the cross at the hands of human beings. However, this reprehensible victimization does not prevent Jesus Christ and God from keeping faith with human beings! God does not will the victimization of Jesus. But God does not allow the fact that human beings and the powers of this world make a victim of Jesus to ruin Jesus' sacrifice and God's care for human beings.

The language of sacrifice emphasizes the fact that God engages the creaturely on its own terms, with its forces and powers. It underlines that God gives the world room for its own development, with the attendant costs and consequences for God. God desires to demonstrate the divine glory precisely in self-giving to us and to persons of other times and regions of the world, precisely in the breadth and depth of this self-giving. In this sense it is correct to speak of the 'suffering God' – and thus not only with regard to the cross.

Reply: Incarnational Reality

JOHN POLKINGHORNE

I very much agree with Michael Welker's concept of 'a dynamic realism'. Only such a concept could be adequate to humanity's unfolding exploration of reality. We see this dynamism in science as quantum theory qualifies and changes the insights of classical Newtonian physics. We see it equally in the continuing Christological quest to do justice to the phenomenon of Jesus Christ.

I am grateful for Michael's emphasis that the cross does not only reveal the crucified God but also the sinfulness of humanity and the distorting influences of the powers of this world. In Christ there is hope for the redemption of society and its powers and authorities, as well as for individuals. Indeed the destinies of both lie together in the Spirit's work of forming the body of Christ. A religion that spoke solely of the eternal victim would no more be true to Christian experience and insight than a religion that spoke solely of impassible deity and invulnerable divine power. No doubt easy dualisms are to be transcended, but the way to that discovery, it seems to me, lies in holding as one the ultimately single event of Calvary and Easter, or better still, the whole incarnation and the whole exaltation of Christ, for I agree that the total life of Jesus is his faithful sacrifice, an insight that perhaps Catholic thinking has preserved better than most Protestant thought.

I prefer the phrase 'the real presence' to the phrase 'the personal presence' of the risen Christ, because I believe that the former conveys better the multi-dimensional character of the eucharistic encounter, with the one who both lived and died for us in Palestine and who is also the one by whom everything was made that was made.

NOTES

1. For a much fuller account of my views, see J. C. Polkinghorne, *Science and Christian Belief/The Faith of a Physicist*, SPCK/Princeton University Press, 1994.
2. See ibid., chs 5–7.
3. See ibid. ch. 6. The fact that the various appearance stories have the unexpected common theme of a difficulty in recognizing the risen Christ, and that the stories of the empty tomb centre on its discovery by women (who were not regarded as valid witnesses in the ancient world), are among details that

persuade me that genuine historical reminiscences lie behind these strands of tradition. See also Michael Welker, Chapter 4.

4. Polkinghorne, *Christian Belief/Faith*, ch. 7.
5. J. C. Polkinghorne, *Belief in God in an Age of Science*, Yale University Press, 1998, ch. 2.
6. J. Moltmann, *The Crucified God*, SCM Press, 1974.
7. J. C. Polkinghorne, *Science and Creation*, SPCK, 1988, p. 97.
8. See The Doctrine Commission of the Church of England, *The Mystery of Salvation*, Church House Publishing, 1995, ch. 5.
9. Polkinghorne, *Christian Belief/Faith*, ch. 9.
10. See J. C. Polkinghorne and M. Welker (eds), *The Ends of the World and the Ends of God*, Trinity Press International, 2000.
11. See, for example, J. C. Polkinghorne, *The Quantum World*, Longman/Princeton University Press, 1984, ch. 7.
12. The ideas of C. G. Jung about the collective unconscious, although contested, may be of relevance here.
13. See Michael Welker, Chapter 4.
14. Sigrid Brandt, *Opfer als Gedächtnis: Auf dem Weg zu einer befreienden theologischen Rede von Opfer*, Lit, 2000, and bibliography.

4

FAITH IN CHRIST

MICHAEL WELKER

Many people, even Christians, have problems with 'faith' in Jesus Christ. Their difficulties arise from the fact that as modern and enlightened people they find it hard to develop an understanding of the *risen* Christ. Nobody can and has to believe in just the pre-Easter Jesus, abstracting from the resurrected Christ. On the basis of the biblical witnesses and of historical deliberations we can certainly find out a good deal about him. We can emphasize and highly estimate his ethical and religious example. But it is only the risen Jesus Christ who brings faith and makes faith necessary to establish a relationship of himself to human beings or a relationship of humans to him, the true human being and true God.

Faith in Christ as Faith in the Resurrected

Faith in the resurrected is woken through a multitude of appearances of the resurrected among his witnesses.[1] After the disaster of the crucifixion and the night of his forsakenness by God and, at least partly, in connection with the discovery of the empty tomb and on the basis of diverse Easter appearances, the certainty materializes in the so-called 'Jesus movement' among the witnesses to Jesus; Jesus Christ has risen. He lives. He is present in the Spirit. He continues to work among us. Faith in the resurrection has nothing to do with the opinion that the pre-Easter Jesus was physically reanimated. That he simply was there again. The resurrection of Jesus is no mere physical reanimation.[2] A 'spiritual body', a 'glorified body' is now present among human beings through the creative power of God, through the power of the Holy Spirit. This spiritual body, this glorified body makes itself present among the witnesses almost like a natural body. This is what some of the accounts of the resurrection say. They tell us that Jesus lets himself be touched, that he breaks the bread, that he even eats before the eyes of the disciples.

However, at the same time all the accounts of the resurrection make it perfectly clear (when they are really grasped in detail) that here we do not deal with a natural body. Jesus enters the circle of disciples in an unmediated way. He steps through walls and doors. He disappears before the eyes of the disciples, that is at the very moment when they recognize him (cf. Luke 24). The appearances of the resurrected are accompanied by doubt. And where the resurrected is in fact recognized the participants in this event are conscious of a theophany, a revelation of God. 'My Lord and my God!' says the unbelieving Thomas when he follows the invitation of the resurrected, 'put out your hand, and place it in my side ...' He does not say, 'Forgive me, Jesus, that I did not recognize you at once.'

The resurrected reveals himself 'in various forms'. These appearances reach from personal encounters which can indeed be confused with a reanimation to appearances of light as they happen to Paul. Along with and in this self-representation of the resurrected, faith 'comes'. A certainty of the presence of Jesus Christ is established which at the same time knows of its own endangerment, of the endangerment of the certainty of the witnesses and also of the endangerment and the limits of their knowledge.

With the presence of the resurrected no mere natural human being or a specific linear biography is present, but the complete *fullness* of the life of the pre-Easter Jesus. The fullness of this life, the richness of his person is now no longer linked to only one place in space and time, like the personal existence of a natural person. The resurrected and exalted Christ becomes present for us in proclamation, in the celebration of the sacrament, in the exegesis of the Scriptures, in the imitation of Christ and in his glorification. Also with regard to him it remains true that we are to 'search for and love God' (cf. Chapter 2), that we are to strive for an ever clearer knowledge of his person and his presence and that we have to follow his instruction and his example. In the same way that faith in the creator engrosses the whole human existence, so does faith in the resurrected involve our whole existence.

Martin Luther in his *Large Catechism* grasped faith in Jesus Christ in the formula, 'I believe that Jesus Christ has become my Lord.'[3] Luther makes it clear that this 'becoming my Lord' is not concerned with the change of abstract conditions of authority and lordship, but with a comprehensive event of liberation. Jesus Christs drives away 'those tyrants and masters of the cane' and replaces them as the 'Lord of life'. Along with him come 'righteousness, all the good and bliss'. We are sheltered and protected by him. He rules us 'through his righteousness, wisdom, power, life and bliss'.[4]

Faith and Change of Lordship

If we want to understand this lordship and the role of faith in this change of lordship and if this change of lordship is not to be grasped as an abstract 'Christ relation', it is important to perceive that the risen Christ is 'not without his followers'. Martin Luther, Karl Barth (at any rate in his late writings[5]) and other important theologians again and again made this very clear. The risen Christ, who reveals himself in appearances to the first witnesses, is as little 'without his followers' as the risen one, who wants to become present in word and sacrament, is without his witnesses. Rather, the risen Jesus Christ wants to take the witnesses into his presence and into his life and, precisely in this way, give them participation in God's life and in life everlasting.

Through his presence and through his workings *the risen Christ renews the relationship of human beings to God. At the same time he renews the interhuman relations of life.*[6] The glorification of God and participation in loving, forgiving and peacemaking mutual acceptance among human beings must not be separated. It is not an abstract idea of God's righteousness or abstract thoughts about God's life and God's love that are decisive, but the experiences faith has of God's righteousness, life and love in the midst of building up and preserving new interhuman relations. God's righteousness, life and love are shaped and specified through the presence of the resurrected. The experiences faith has of these relations of love, righteousness and life are experiences of relations *owed* to the workings of God. The experience of renewed relations to God and among human beings is characteristic of faith in the resurrected. This connection of the relation to God and of relations among human beings, of reconciliation with God and reconciliation among human beings, is complex. This complex connection can only be grasped in faith, that is in a knowledge that does not only know of these relations, their renewal and their connection, but also of the limits of the inherent individual and common certainty and of the limits of this certainty that are to be transcended again and again.

A comprehensive relation of the individual and communal life before God is given with faith in Jesus Christ. Paul describes this *not only subjective, but also objective faith* very clearly, when at the beginning of his letters he thanks God for the faith of the community 'which is proclaimed in all the world', when he is glad about this faith, when he praises the radiance of this faith and when he says that he would like to participate in this faith or that he would like to strengthen the faith and would like to experience being strengthened through the faith of the communities or of single Christians.[7] But this objectivity of communal faith is grounded in the spiritual objectivity of faith that 'has come with Christ', as Paul says (Galatians 3.23ff.).

It is not only the fullness of the presence of the pre-Easter Jesus in the presence of the resurrected and the fullness of relations on which his presence has a shaping effect that makes us refer to him 'in faith'. It is not only the complex connection of the relation to God and the relations of human beings among each other that transcends our certainty and our knowledge and makes it necessary for us to talk of a 'faith relation' to it. It is not only the individual and the communal being involved in these relations that requires the talk of 'faith' which is more than knowledge and certainty and which at the same time includes knowledge and certainty. Rather, in faith, and in faith only, a set of principal relations, a set of *principally different basic relations to the risen Jesus Christ* are given. We have to make these basic relations and their interconnections clear to ourselves. Only with regard to them does it become obvious what we owe the risen Christ, his workings and his life 'for us'.

Faith and Canonic Remembrance

On the one hand, with the resurrected the '*remembrance*' of the pre-Easter Jesus is given. The remembrance is not a mere recollection, but also an *experience and an expectation* which are deeply influenced by the appearance, the workings and the proclamation of the pre-Easter Jesus. I have termed this remembrance a 'canonic remembrance'[8] because it is formed by the canonical witnesses that mediate to us a specific and limited pluralism of perspectives on the pre-Easter Jesus. It is exactly in this dynamic connection of the various perspectives that we are enabled to realize his living presence. It is the canonic remembrance that shapes a relation to Jesus Christ which is constantly in search of knowledge and renews the readiness to discipleship and witness. It is the canonic remembrance that shapes a relation to Jesus Christ 'in faith'.

The relation in the living canonical remembrance to the pre-Easter Jesus is certainly not an unbroken relation. The remembrance established for Jesus Christ is not only like the monumental memory established for historical heroes and rulers. In the memory of the 'night of betrayal' and the 'proclamation of his death' the remembrance of Jesus Christ is connected with the experience that all the world shut itself off from this remembrance and from the knowledge of the revelation of God in Jesus Christ and does so again and again. The faith in Jesus Christ is threatened by unbelief, by the breaking off of all salvific expectations which have linked themselves to his person. Faith is threatened through the failure of the religious, political, legal and moral forms and achievements, through the failure of the 'powers of this world', the natural and cultural powers of life over against the presence of God. Faith in Jesus Christ is threatened by chaos, by terror, and by the wretched suffering that the biblical traditions call 'sin'.[9]

Against disbelief, even from disbelief, God establishes, raises and animates faith in the resurrected. This is the situation from which Christ himself gathered his witnesses, from which he makes a new beginning in the midst of a creation that suffers from the power of sin. It is only in faith, only in a certainty again and again broken and endangered, only in a knowledge again and again broken and endangered, that we can relate to the resurrected if we grasp in him also the crucified one and, along with the cross, the sin of the world or the world under the power of sin. In the crucified Christ we encounter the God who bestows upon us the divine love and mercy until death, even to the experience of hell. The crucified Christ gives us the hope that we cannot fall any deeper than into God's hand. He gives us the hope that no power can separate us from God's love. He gives us the strength to perceive and to bear the ambivalences and darknesses of creation and, beyond that, the terror and the chaos in creation under the power of sin.

As soon as we understand God's good intentions with creation and also the endangerment of creation, as soon as we understand Christ's turning to the lost human being and also the persistence of their opposition to the divine love, it becomes inescapably clear that God's reign is only in the coming and that the risen and exalted Christ still goes to meet his complete representation, his parousia. Also in this respect we can and must speak of a 'believing' relation to the resurrected and elevated one, of a faith and a hope in which we live and look forward to the coming Christ, the coming merciful judge of the world, the coming saviour.[10] At the same time it becomes inescapably clear that the coming Christ is the one who also comes to *us*, who approaches *us*, but that he must not be considered the saviour who *only* works in *our* time and in *our* world, in *our* church. The coming Jesus Christ is the Lord of all times and worlds. His revelation in fullness, his parousia, goes along with the passing of heaven and earth, a transformation of history,[11] a fulfilment of the world which necessarily transcends all our ideas of world, reality and temporality. Only in faith can we refer to this reality.

Faith by which God Elevates and Ennobles Us

The eschatological view is not an earthly looking, but an 'understanding, even as I have been fully understood', an attempt to understand with God's eyes. Faith in the resurrected thus is in various ways wider than knowledge.[12] For several reasons, it is a certainty and a knowledge and at the same time a knowledge of the endangerment of certainty and the limits of knowledge.

1. Faith in the resurrected is a living relation to the resurrected, to the fullness of his life.
2. In faith in the resurrected, we are concerned with living relations in the community of the believers who constitute the body of Christ, the body of the post-Easter Jesus Christ.
3. It is the complex relation of faith which brings together the living relation to God and the living relations among the believers, a connection that we cannot exhaust with our knowledge and our certainty.
4. We are concerned with a relation of 'faith', since the individual self-relation of the believer has to correspond to the condition of objective faith and thus is correspondingly complex.
5. The above-mentioned relations gain their profile in that God's workings in the face of the power of sin in the world are perceived above all in Jesus Christ's crucifixion and resurrection.

    Faith in Christ gains its profile in that on the cross the 'sin of the world', the lostness of the world and of human beings, and their being in need of God, become revealed, and in that through the resurrection, God's dealing with the world's resistance against his presence and goodness becomes known. With regard to cross and resurrection we recognize God's fathomless faithfulness. This faithfulness cannot be blocked by the fact that human beings try to obstruct God's sacrifice. Even their victimizing the crucified cannot put an end to God's faithfulness and sacrifice and turn it into an absurdity. In faith, however, this abyss of human existence, with its lostness, its deep brokenness and its greatest endangerment becomes evident. In faith, we can face the power of sin which presses us to live our lives without God's presence and help.

6. Finally, in faith also the exaltation becomes obvious that God grants to humans by which God elevates and ennobles lost human beings.

Faith as Hope for Creation

What in the chapter about faith in God the creator we – perhaps a little daringly – termed 'a growing of God beyond Godself' becomes clear in faith in the resurrected. God does not only restore and keep the endangered creation through the resurrection and the involvement of the witnesses in the life of the resurrected. Bread and wine in the Lord's Supper are not only good gifts of creation, gifts likewise of nature and of the cultural cooperation of human beings. Bread and wine in holy communion become recognizable before the background of the night of betrayal and of the cross and in the context of the resurrection as '*gifts of the new creation*'. They are gifts through which God lets us participate in the life of the resurrected and thus in God's eternal life.

Here human beings are given faith experience of the elevation of creatures, the experience that we are destined and renewed to represent the *imago Dei*, the image of God on earth. Human beings are given faith experience of the dignity that is bestowed on them and faith experience that they are meant to have participation in an indestructible eternal life, in the divine life. These experiences can only be accepted in a knowledge and a certainty which precisely as certainty of faith opens up towards truth, which time and again searches for the knowledge of God and is ready and willing to renew its own relation to God or rather have it renewed.

Faith in the resurrected is deeply connected with faith in God the creator. In the resurrection the shaping, judging and saving power; the personal will which keeps together nature, culture and history, and in all this, our lives; and the personal instance which directs the creaturely being and life and gives it its meaning, direction and destination, becomes revealed. With regard to the resurrected the workings of the creative God gain a clarity which cannot be attained in relation to the creator and to creation on their own (cf. Chapters 1 and 2). A great number of questions which the mere knowledge of creation is not able to answer are answered through God's revelation in Christ. God intends to have the creatures gain participation in divine life. They are to participate in the *divine life*; as *creatures* they are to gain participation in the divine life. Therefore God creates non-divine existences. Therefore God risks a difference to God and with it resistance towards the divine, the refusal, endangerment and compromising of the divine intentions. Therefore God becomes vulnerable and goes into suffering and death. Creaturely life is to have participation in the divine life. This destination, this elevation, this appreciation of creaturely life can only be known and experienced with regard to the second Person of the Trinity, the resurrected, his person, his activity and his presence.

At the same time the question remains open *how* this activity claims us, how this power works on us, how we can enter into a living relationship with this personal instance. In which way is our life, through the creative God and the presence of the resurrected Christ, given a sense, a direction and a destination in the great powers of nature, culture and history? In which way are the activity of the creator and the workings of the resurrected for our benefit? At this point we have arrived at the question: What does faith in God the Spirit mean?

Comments: Witness to the Risen Christ
JOHN POLKINGHORNE

For both of us, the resurrection of Jesus Christ plays a pivotal role in our understanding of Christian truth. Indeed, it is essential to the possibility of our embracing that truth. In accordance with the kind of apologetic concerns to which I have already confessed, I placed an emphasis on the evidential character of the resurrection, as affirming God's positive resolution of the ambiguity otherwise inherent in the event of the crucifixion of Jesus of Nazareth. I also used the scandal of its particularity to illustrate, and then defend, the necessity of the unique in any revelatory encounter of a personal kind.

Once again I am very grateful to Michael Welker for the way in which his chapter widens and deepens the context within which I can place my own reflections. I have found particularly illuminating his emphasis on the indispensable role of the witnesses and on the simultaneously objective and subjective character of encounters with the risen Christ, who both appears in bodily form, bearing the scars of the passion, and yet is also elusively hard to recognize, even though hearts burn within when in conversation with him. These insights afford us important links between the unrepeatable foundational experiences of the apostolic witnesses and the continuing testimony of generations of subsequent believers who still confess that 'Jesus lives!' There must be these resonances within our present experience to a degree sufficient to make credible, in a living way, the accounts of the apostolic experiences. One such resonance occurs in the believer's experience of the real but hidden presence of Christ in the eucharistic offering of gifts of bread and wine 'that earth has given and human hands have made'.

For me, the central illuminating passage in relation to the nature of faith is when Michael writes,

> *Faith in Jesus Christ is threatened by chaos, by terror, and by the wretched suffering that the biblical traditions call 'sin'. Against disbelief, even from disbelief, God establishes, raises and animates faith in the resurrected. ... It is only in faith, only in a certainty again and again broken and endangered, only in a knowledge again and again broken and endangered, that we can relate to the resurrected if we grasp in him also the crucified one and, along with the cross, the sin of the world or the world under the power of sin.*

We return here to the theme of the necessity of a balance between boldness and careful self-criticism in our human search for truth, so that we succumb neither to rashness nor to despair in the quest. Ultimately, Christian truth is to be found in a person and not in propositions. We recognize that faith demands the total response of heart and will, as well as assent of the mind, so that awe and worship and obedience are indispensable elements in our encounter with the risen Christ. We live in the midst of many and great dangers, but the crucified and risen Lord is the living assurance for us of the invincible and loving faithfulness of God. Like the man in the Gospel, we cry out, 'I believe; help my unbelief!' (Mark 9.24).

Reply: 'A Balance Between Boldness and Careful Self-Criticism'

MICHAEL WELKER

I became intrigued by the subtlety of the biblical resurrection accounts which finds an expression in the display of balance between boldness and careful self-criticism. Proskynesis, *prostration in the face of the theophany, and the comment, 'But some doubted', is characteristic of the witnesses to the reality of the resurrection. The fact is interesting, too, that spectacular revelations like the angelic appearances at the empty tomb in themselves do not yet lead to the proclamation: 'Christ is risen.' The stories of the empty tomb in themselves lead to fear and silence (Mark), to the comment, 'It is just the talk of women' (Luke), to the propaganda, 'the body has been stolen', or to the worry evoked by this event (Matthew and John). There is the secondary perspective in Luke and John that Peter goes home in amazement and that the 'other disciple' starts to believe before all the others do so; but this is obviously not sufficient to spread the resurrection belief. The resurrection belief is ignited in a much more modest way, indeed, out of a multiplicity of modest experiences of the witnesses. They lead to the bold proclamation in the midst of fear and doubt. Truth and mere certainty are constantly differentiated. A community of witnesses is established, a 'truth-seeking community', as John Polkinghorne named it.*

The breaking of bread, the opening of the Scriptures, formulas of address and encounters of a very simple kind lead to the acknowledgement of the divine act and the revelation of the resurrected. The Emmaus story in Luke 24 is particularly revealing in this respect:

- *The eyes of the disciples are held;*
- *then the breaking of bread opens their eyes;*
- *then the resurrected disappears before their eyes;*
- *but instead of bemoaning a spooky event, they remember that they had another experience of evidence which did not yet lead to the testimony of the resurrection;*
- *namely the opening of the Scriptures.*

So two very basic experiences are decisive for the recognition of a revelation of God: boldness and cautious and careful self-criticism, multiple and diverse, affirmed and questioned experiences of faith evidence lead to the proclamation of the resurrection that is crucial for faith in Christ.

NOTES
1. For a more detailed account cf. M. Welker, 'Resurrection and Eternal Life: The Canonic Memory of the Resurrected Christ, His Reality, and His Glory', in J. Polkinghorne and M. Welker (eds), *The End of the World and the Ends of God*, Trinity Press International, 2000; 'Resurrection and the Reign of God, The 1993 Frederick Neumann Symposium on the Theological Interpretation of Scripture: Hope for the Kingdom and Responsibility for the World', *The Princeton Seminary Bulletin*, Supplementary Issue, No. 3, ed. Daniel Migliore, Princeton, 1994, pp. 3–16.
2. Jesus' restoration to life is not to be confused with the limits of the wonders of healing as they are narrated under the title of 'resuscitation' of Jairus' daughter (Mark 5 and Luke 8) and of Lazarus (John 11f.).
3. *Luther's Large Catechism*, Anniversary Translation, Luther Publishing House, 1983.
4. Ibid.
5. *Church Dogmatics*, IV.
6. I have elaborated this connection of what theologians like to call 'vertical dimension' and 'horizontal dimension' in my book *What Happens in Holy Communion?*, trans. John Hoffmeyer, Eerdmans and SPCK, 2000, esp. ch. 3.
7. In the first chapter of Romans, Paul clearly describes a complex spiritual exchange as 'faith': 'First, I thank my God through Jesus Christ for all of you, *because your faith is proclaimed throughout the world* ... For I am longing to see you so that I may share with you some spiritual gift to strengthen you – or rather so that we *may be mutually encouraged by each other's faith, both yours and mine*' (Romans 1.8, 11–12). Paul also shares with the Thessalonians, at the beginning of the first of his letters to them: 'In every place your faith in God has become known' (1 Thessalonians 1.8). He announces that he will send Timothy as a messenger to 'strengthen ... you for the sake of your faith' and 'to find out about your faith'. Finally, he tells them that he rejoices over 'the good news of your faith' (1 Thessalonians 3.2–6, cf. 7ff. and 2 Thessalonians 1.3). But not only in Paul's writings do we find formulations that make thankful reference to the fact that the faith of a community is publicly known (cf. Colossians 1.4; Ephesians 1.15; Hebrews 13.1). In Philemon and 2 Timothy the same thing occurs with regard to the faith of individuals that has 'become known' (cf. Philemon 1.5; 2 Timothy 1.5).
8. Cf. Polkinghorne and Welker, *The End of the World and the Ends of God*, n. 1.
9. Cf. in detail, Welker, *What Happens in Holy Communion?*, esp. chs 2 and 6–8.
10. Cf. J. Moltmann, *Der Weg Jesu Christi. Christologie in messianischen Dimensionen*, Kaiser, 1989.
11. In the sense of Hegel's *Aufhebung*, as both elimination and being kept and saved on a different level.
12. Cf. John Polkinghorne's differentiation between explanation and understanding, in *Science and Christian Belief/The Faith of a Physicist*, SPCK/Princeton University Press, 1994, pp. 36ff.; see also Nicholas of Cusa, *De docta ignorantia* of 1440.

5

FAITH IN THE HOLY SPIRIT

JOHN POLKINGHORNE

Whatever orthodoxy may say, many Christians are effectively binitarians. God the Father, and Jesus Christ the Son, are concepts with which we can wrestle, but the Spirit so often seems to elude our grasp, as if we sought to clutch at the wind, which can also be the meaning of the Greek and Hebrew words for spirit.

The Hidden Spirit

In translations of the New Testament we are often unsure whether to write spirit or Spirit. In the Apostles' Creed, after the first two articles, the Spirit receives only a brief explicit mention, though we can see the clauses that follow, relating to the life of the Church and the hope of the life to come, as constituting also implicit recognitions of the Spirit's working. Even the Nicene-Constantinopolitan Creed of 381 exercises some degree of constraint in describing the Third Person as 'the Lord and giver of life' but not using the *homoousion* language applied to the Second Person. In pictorial representations of the Trinity, at least in the tradition of the Western Church, the modest figure of the dove contrasts with the imposing personal figures of the kingly Father and the crucified Son. Sometimes even this degree of manifest presence of the Spirit is lacking, as in the medieval carving in the St Calixtus Chapel of Wells Cathedral. The iconography of the Eastern Church is more visibly satisfactory in its use of the three angelic figures of the Old Testament Trinity.

Among congregations affected by the charismatic movement, however, there does seem to be a much more active awareness of the manifestations of the Spirit. Here pneumatic hiddenness and self-effacement give way to an altogether more exuberant expression of the

Spirit's working. One has to ask whether these are the full and authentic consequences that ought to follow from faith in the Holy Spirit, and whether the vagueness and perplexity felt elsewhere in the Church are signs of a lack of such faith. There are certainly Pentecostal Christians who would make that judgement. However, it will be a principal thesis of this chapter that hiddenness is a characteristic property of the Spirit and that, if the Spirit is to be known in accordance with the pneumatic nature, then an inescapable degree of veiledness will be involved. Once again, our knowledge must be conformed to the nature of the One we seek to know.

Orthodox Christianity has expressed this insight in a graphic way by its concept of the images of the divine Persons. According to the Eastern Church, the Father's image is manifested in the Son, and the Son's image is manifested in the Spirit, but the Spirit in this age is only secretly manifested by the ultimate work of creating the pneumatic image in the company of sanctified believers, an image that will only be manifested overtly at the end of time.[1] This eschatological fulfilment of the Spirit's work, creating and eventually exhibiting the ranks of the redeemed, by no means implies that the contemporary working of the Spirit is confined within the limits of the visible Church. In fact, faith in the Holy Spirit is a powerful way of understanding the immanent activity of the divine throughout the whole created order.

The Activity of the Spirit

At the risk of seeming to compartmentalize what is fundamentally one, it will be convenient initially to explore the universal activity of the Spirit under three headings that make some degree of discrimination about the nature of this action. This is because the Spirit is a divine Person, acting in different ways in different circumstances, and not an undifferentiated divine force.

(1) *The Spirit and the company of Christian believers.* At Pentecost, the Spirit is pictured as descending on the disciples with the sound of a mighty rushing wind and in tongues of fire 'distributed and resting on each one of them' (Acts 2.3). While the image of the wind suggests the presence of overwhelming power, the image of the individual tongues of fire tempers this by suggesting the particularity of the Spirit's working in relation to each disciple. In 1 Corinthians, Paul speaks of the 'varieties of

gifts' (12.4), emphasizing as he lists them that they originate from 'the same Spirit' and that different people are given different gifts. These gifts are by no means limited to the spectacular charisms valued within the Pentecostal tradition, though these are not excluded either. (Paul's lists include 'tongues' – the action of the Spirit is not to be confined to the conventionally decorous.) It was surely this pneumatic discretion, in which the Spirit 'apportions to each one individually as he wills' (1 Corinthians 12.11), that was one of the reasons that led the Church to realize that the Spirit was to be spoken of as a divine Person and not simply as an impersonal manifestation of divine power.

The hiddenness of the Spirit is also consonant with the experience of many believers. One of the paradoxes of the Christian life is the interplay of divine grace and human free will. 'Work out your own salvation with fear and trembling; for God is at work in you' (Philippians 2.12–13). This paradox is not only a profound theological conundrum, but it is also a fact of Christian experience. Particularly as we face the future, we are conscious of our powers of decision and the responsibilities that they imply we bear for our actions. Particularly as we look back on our lives, we are conscious how God has guided us. This guidance may often have been in unspectacular ways, the nudge of an opportunity offered and taken is frequently the form it takes. The believer will be able to see in this the gentle promptings of the Spirit, hiddenly at work.

This secret character of the Spirit's activity obviously intensifies the epistemological problems with which we have been so concerned. Discernment of the Spirit has some analogy with the discernment of human character. Tacit skills of empathetic understanding are required in both cases and the motivations for belief will be too subtle for any unproblematic appeal to absolutely certain judgement. In engagement with reality, there is no escape from some degree of ambiguity in the realm of the personal.

(2) *The Spirit and the inhabited world.* The God of all the Earth will surely not have left the divine nature without witness or experienced presence at any time or in any place. The Spirit will be engaged with all human beings in appropriate ways, but we may expect there to be differences in the manner in which this happens, and in the way in which it is described, between those who name the name of Christ and those who do not do so.

The bewildering variety of the world faith traditions, and the cognitive dissonance that one finds between them, is a greatly perplexing and a greatly important problem faced by contemporary theology.[2] Amid all the confusion, it is still possible to recognize that testimony is being borne by all the traditions to some form of encounter with what we may call the dimension of the sacred. For the Christian theologian, this can be interpreted as a sign of the Spirit's veiled working within the manifold cultural contexts of humanity. Indeed, the concept of the Spirit, immanently present to creation, seems to offer Christian theology its most promising resource for a respectful approach to other faiths. This way of understanding will not deny the reality of other religions' encounters with the sacred, nor the presence of salvific experience within the lives of their followers, but it will see these as hidden fruits of the unnamed Spirit. Thus it is possible for the Christian to acknowledge the authenticity of others' experience, without denying those unique aspects of Christian understanding of the divine nature that have to be held as non-negotiable by the believer.

The clearest example to consider is provided by the role of the Spirit in the life of Israel and in the continuing life of Judaism. Of course the Spirit did not come into being, or move into action for the first time, at the Christian Pentecost. What had previously been experienced in a more implicit mode was then experienced more explicitly, not least because it was now possible to identify the Spirit as 'the Spirit of Christ' (Romans 8.9). In the Hebrew Bible, the personal character of the Spirit is less clearly perceptible, though it may be seen in the 'still small voice' that spoke to Elijah at the mouth of the cave after the violent wind and the earthquake and the fire (1 Kings 20.12). The hiddenness and ambiguity of the workings of the Spirit, with consequent possibilities for deviation and error, may also seem to be conveyed in this passage. Reference to the swords of Hazael, Jehu and Elisha recall those acts of war and genocide which are so plentifully present in the Old Testament, but which we have difficulty in seeing as expressions of God's will.

Vulnerability to the distortion of the promptings of the Spirit did not come to an end at Pentecost, as the tale of the persecutions, pogroms and crusades that mar the history of the Church makes only too obvious. The presence of the Spirit does not overwhelm individuals, as if the purpose of its bestowal were to produce divinely programmed automata. When the temperate Anglican bishop of Durham, Joseph Butler, said to John Wesley, 'Sir, pretending to extraordinary revelations and gifts of the Holy Ghost is a horrid thing, a very horrid thing', he may have been exhibiting the limitations of an eighteenth-century, coolly rational approach to religion, but he was also pointing to a possible source of spiritual danger. Faith in the Holy Spirit requires the exercise of the gift of discernment. 'Do not quench the Spirit, do not despise prophesying, but test everything; hold fast what is good, abstain from every form of evil' (1 Thessalonians 5.19–21).

(3) *The Spirit and the whole of creation.* According to Genesis 1.2, the Spirit of God hovered over the face of the waters of chaos at the beginning of creation. Or was it 'the wind of God' that blew across the primordial deep? The ambiguity of the word *ruach* permits either translation. Such uncertainty is consonant with the way in which people may think about the unfolding fruitful history of cosmic and terrestrial evolution. A theologian will wish to interpret the story as *creatio continua*, a continuously unfolding expression of the creator's will.[3] That will partly finds its expression in the autopoietic powers of self-organization with which God has endowed matter. While to the atheist this will seem no more than natural process at work, to the theist the astonishing fruitfulness of that process will be understood as an expression of the purposes of the ordainer of nature's laws. In theological terms, this is the *Logos* aspect of creation. In scientific terms, it is the necessity aspect of the evolutionary interplay between chance and necessity that is here being manifested. Yet if the term *creatio continua* is to carry its proper meaning, the activity of God cannot be wholly absent from the chance side of that interplay as well. Surely God must participate providentially in the contingencies of history. Christian theology does not treat the universe as being God's puppet theatre, for there is a genuine openness within which creatures are allowed to be and to make themselves, but it is not a world whose creator is a deistic absentee landlord either. A theistic view of evolution can expect the Spirit to be secretly at work, guiding cosmic history through hidden action, concealed within the cloudy unpredictabilities with which the physical world abounds.[4]

But there is also another, and a more profound, aspect to the Spirit's relationship with creation. An evolutionary universe is a world with an inevitable cost in extinctions and malformations, as the creaturely explorations of potentiality run into blind alleys or fail in other ways. Within such a process, death is the necessary cost of new life. Many sensitive people, including Darwin himself, have questioned whether so painful a history could be the expression of the will of a benevolent creator. In one of the most astonishing passages in the whole of the New Testament, Paul has something to say that is very relevant to this issue:

> We know that the whole creation has been groaning (*sustenazei*) in travail together until now; and not only the creation, but we ourselves, who have the first fruits of the Spirit, groan (*stenazomen*) inwardly as we wait for adoption as sons, the redemption of our bodies ... Likewise the Spirit helps us in our weakness, for we do not know how to pray as we ought, but the Spirit himself intercedes for us with sighs (*stenagmois*) too deep for words. (Romans 8.22–3 and 26)

In other words, there is indeed a passion that creation is undergoing before its eschatological redemption, *and the Spirit is party to that passion*. Here once more we see how essential it is to understand the Holy Spirit in terms that are profoundly personal and not merely those of impersonal power. The Christian God is a 'fellow sufferer who understands' not only because of divine participation in the life and death of Jesus Christ, but also because faith in the Spirit involves a belief in the Spirit's continued sharing in the travail of creation.

The Presence of the Spirit

We have considered three different aspects of the immanent working of the Holy Spirit. Because experience of the Spirit involves encounter with God in the divine immanence, there is universal pneumatic activity within the order of creation. Yet we have seen that this does not at all imply that its character is uniform and unaffected by the particularity of circumstances. Because the Spirit is a divine Person this could not be so but, on the contrary, action will be perfectly attuned to the individuality of each happening, responsive to each acknowledged need. The Spirit will be respectful of the divinely granted creaturely independence. The Spirit will share in each moment of suffering and loss.

Where there are those who are seeking to be open and responsive to the divine will, the Spirit will be experienced as a gracious presence, empowering the discernment and fulfilment of that purpose. Where there is painful travail, the Spirit will be there participating in that passion with groanings too profound for ordinary utterance. Where there are those who rebel against God and defy the divine will, the Spirit will be a pleading presence, seeking to recover the lost but not imposing irresistibly upon them. Such creaturely exclusions of 'the Lord and Giver of life', if persisted in, threaten mortal consequences. 'When thou hidest thy face, they are dismayed; when thou takest away their breath (*ruach*), they die and return to their dust' (Psalm 104.29). We must surely understand talk of God's taking away the Holy Spirit not as abandonment and withdrawal of the divine mercy, but as a sorrowful acquiescence in creaturely persistence in defiance and rejection. The state of life in which God has been deliberately and unremittingly kept at bay is the state we rightly call hell, a state of dreariness on the brink of non-being. Humans do not possess an intrinsic immortality, and our hope of a destiny beyond death depends on the faithfulness and power of God alone. Where that power is excluded and that faithfulness spurned, eternal life is being rejected.

In its worshipping life, the Church acknowledges the operation of the Spirit throughout the created order. In many liturgies, both ancient and modern, there is a twofold *epiclesis* (calling down of the Holy Spirit) as part of the eucharistic prayer of thanksgiving. The presence of the Spirit is invoked both upon the gifts of bread and wine, 'which earth has given and human hands have made' – the fruits of nature and of human culture – and also on the gathered community of the faithful. The presence of the Spirit is not confined to humanity alone.

Within the life of the Church, the role of the Spirit also includes that of being the prime witness to Christ. The Johannine way of speaking about the Spirit laid considerable emphasis on a continuing pneumatological role in relation to revelation and to the appropriation of truth about God. In the great discourse in the upper room, Jesus says, 'I have yet many things to say to you, but you cannot bear them now. When the Spirit of truth comes, he will guide you into all the truth; for he will not speak on his own authority, but whatever he hears he will speak, and he will declare to you the things that are to come' (John 16.12–13). Faith in the Spirit implies a belief in divine guidance at work in the formation of the New Testament writings as they arose from the testimonies of proclamation and the oral tradition, in the eventual selection of the canon, and in the continuing understanding and interpretation of Scripture. The Spirit has indeed 'spoken by the prophets', but the Spirit did not then fall silent but rather continues to speak. We must expect there to have been development of doctrine, whether it be through the Trinitarian and Christological deliberations of Nicaea and Chalcedon, through the effects of Reformation and Counter-Reformation, or just through continuous theological reflection down the centuries. Of course, the protocols against distortion and deception continue to operate. There is no infallibility guaranteed to church, council or patriarch. There are also conditions of diachronic consonance that must be satisfied. These do not deny the possibility of new insight, but they require it to bear some recognizable relationship to the insight of the past, if it is to be truly the Spirit of Christ who has inspired the new understanding.

The Spirit of truth will be at work not only in religious communities, but also within all truth-seeking communities, of whatever kind. This will surely include the community of scientists. There is a well-documented experience that often accompanies significant discoveries, whether in mathematics or in natural science. First, there is an intense engagement with the problem, involving long wrestling with the facts and ideas as they stand at that time. In the end, this may lead simply to frustration and bafflement. If that is the case, a fallow period, in which the perplexities are consciously set aside and engagement with the problem suspended, is the next step. It may then happen – obviously not every time, but sufficiently often to be significant – that the solution to the problem arises spontaneously and unbidden in the mind of the investigator. Some new complex idea may be grasped immediately and as a whole, though perhaps requiring many weeks of subsequent working out in respect to its details. Such moments of illumination are self-authenticating in their immediate persuasiveness, and those who experience them frequently speak of them as being 'given'. No doubt the activity of the unconscious mind plays an important part in what has been going on, but the believer may well wish to suppose that the hidden inspiration of the Spirit has also been involved in bringing new insight. Even more readily may one suppose this to be the case in the creative moments of the artist, which are often described by those who experience them as being moments of gift.

The Human Spirit

The fact that this chapter is somewhat briefer than my previous two is itself a testimony to the hidden elusiveness of the Spirit. We have been less concerned than before with appeals to itemized evidence and more involved in general theological discussion. In consequence, some of the arguments may have seemed somewhat tenuous and vulnerable to alternative interpretation, as if they were no more than pious perspectives on what in reality might be no more than secular process. To demand greater transparency and definiteness would be to do violence to the nature of the One of whom it was said, 'The wind blows where it wills, and you hear the sound of it, but you do not know whence it comes or whither it goes; so it is with everyone who is born of the Spirit' (John 3.8).

Finally, we must acknowledge that for many of our contemporaries, deeply impressed by the success of a physicalist and reductionist science in gaining understanding of so many aspects of our embodied existence, it may be difficult to take seriously any idea of a human dimension of the spiritual, let alone the existence of the divine Spirit. They would be tempted to dismiss our discussion as, at best, epiphenomenal, at worst, fantastic. However, even within physical science itself there is a hint of an insight pointing beyond a merely matter–energy account of reality.

The advent of considerable computing power has made it possible to make a beginning of the study of complex systems. Much of the work so far has been of a natural history kind, depending upon investigation of computer-generated models of systems and the properties that their emulations display. It is becoming increasingly clear that systems of this kind are capable of generating a quite astonishing degree of pattern in their overall behaviour, of a previously unsuspected kind.[5] In other words, their adequate description seems to require not only the kind of energetic interactions between their constituents with which physics has long been familiar, but also some complementary holistic account that deals with the kind of patterning expressive of order-creating information. There is currently no known general theory that undergirds and interprets this new kind of behaviour, but doubtless the infant science of complexity theory will one day lead to the discovery of such principles. At present, all that one can say is that there is strong encouragement to believe that for complex systems the causal principles at work will include not only the atomized effects of matter–energy interactions, but also a new principle that one could, in view of its pattern-forming propensities, call 'active information'. Putting the matter in a different way, we appear to have to conceive not only of the bottom-up causalities exerted by the parts upon the whole, but also of a top-down causality of the whole, acting upon the parts.

Notions of this kind have encouraged some thought, necessarily speculative and incomplete, in relation to the exercise of agency, both human and divinely providential.[6] There is also a faint glimmer of light towards what might eventually prove to be a concept of the creaturely dimension of spirit, understood in non-dualist terms because related to embodied being. Human beings are more than computers made of meat, and our minds are more than software running on the hardware of our brains.[7] Active information is an idea that may give a hint of the deliverance of science from the temptation of a crass materialism. It might prove to be a straw in a wind blown by the Spirit.

Comments: The Working of the Spirit 'From Below' and 'From Above'
MICHAEL WELKER

In Christology, many theologians differentiate between 'Christologies from below', which start with the historical Jesus and with the humanity of Jesus Christ, and 'Christologies from above', which start with the resurrected and elevated Christ and his divinity. In the doctrine of the Holy Spirit we again have to do with these dimensions. In my book on the Holy Spirit I was very much concerned with the notion of the 'pouring of the Spirit', the Spirit's working 'from above'. Yet I was quite sceptical of metaphysical concepts of the Spirit, particularly of those working too easily with an omni-quantor which makes the Spirit the cause of 'everything'. In several respects John Polkinghorne's contribution on the Holy Spirit challenged me to rethink my sceptical view.

Omnicausing, omnipresent, omnipotent

His contribution caused me to differentiate between

- *the 'omnipotence' of the Spirit, which has to be affirmed if we do not want to contradict a verse like Psalm 139.7: 'Whither shall I go from thy Spirit? . . .', and*
- *the idea of the 'omnicausing' Spirit, which has to be rejected if we take other scriptural witnesses like 1 Thessalonians 5.19; Ephesians 4.30 seriously.*

With this differentiation we can maintain a qualified understanding of the 'omnipresence'. Despite this clarification I should like to emphasize that in my view theology should work very cautiously with the metaphysical omni-concept. It often seems to put us on 'safe' religious grounds, but in fact easily blurs the workings of the living God.

I also welcome the interpretation of the 'tongues of fire' which left me clueless when I wrote my book on the Holy Spirit. Like in the revelation of God in the burning bush, this fire is not destructive, but rather creative. It illuminates and ennobles individual creatures, as John points out. At the same time it unites a group of human beings so that they can be recognized and recognize each other as – in the words of the young Schleiermacher – 'the forsworn in favour of a better world'.

The Spirit as 'the fellow-sufferer, who understands'?

Another challenge of this chapter was the challenge to understand the 'personhood' of the Spirit by focusing on the encounter of the Spirit with creatures. When I worked on the pneumatology of the biblical traditions it became utterly clear to me that the Holy Spirit cannot be understood as a self-referential person – a point that the influential concepts of 'Spirit' developed by Aristotle and Hegel seem to miss. I tried to understand the personhood of the Holy Spirit as the 'public person' and the 'field of resonance' of Christ. John Polkinghorne points toward a dimension that I will have to explore more thoroughly. In our conversations he called this dimension 'the working of the Spirit from below'. It seems to me that A. N. Whitehead's often-quoted statement 'God is the fellow-sufferer, who understands' could very well express this dimension of the Spirit.

The Spirit and the discernment of distortive and creative differences

Probably more easily than John, I would embrace the relation of creativity and difference. 'The bewildering variety of the world faith traditions' indeed offers us pictures of 'dissonance' and 'confusion'. But if we can discern common or analogous concerns, symbols and figures of thought or at least clear contrasts, the same variety also provides us with valuable differences which challenge us and lead us to a deeper understanding of God and God's creation. The differentiation of differences seems to be very important in cultures that are still very much influenced by a modern rationality and its liberal drive toward 'integration'.

In my view, we need to discern

- *distortive, even demonic differences, that should definitely be overcome, but might be too powerful over against human strivings alone;*
- *form-giving and orienting differences; some of them can be very hard to bear but are nevertheless most important – like the tension between the 'call to dominion' and the* imago dei;
- *differences that help us to challenge and transform our intellectual and moral certainties and guide us towards truth and righteousness; and*
- *creative differences in which we can simply rejoice.*

I think that the creative Holy Spirit, who frees us from sin, constitutes community, restores our lives and keeps us for eternal life, works on all these levels.

Finally, I do agree that the concentration on the Spirit and the Spirit's workings can offer bridges to other traditions of faith and also to secular mindsets, especially when we focus on the relation of 'the law and the Spirit'. This field, it seems to me, is one of the most promising areas of further exploration between the natural sciences, the cultural sciences and theology.

Reply: The Personhood of the Spirit
JOHN POLKINGHORNE

Both Michael Welker and I are anxious to emphasize the personal character of the Spirit and so deliver theological thinking from mere notions of power and of a kind of diffuse and 'ghostly' presence. I think, therefore, that his warning of the metaphysical impersonality that can lurk in 'omni' language is to be heeded. Yet one should not place any part of creation outside the merciful presence of the divine Spirit, however appropriately differentiated the character of that presence must be if it is to be expressed in accordance with the particularity of the situation. When I look at the activity of the Spirit in the world's many sacred communities, I still remain more puzzled, and disconcerted, than Michael by the extraordinary breadth of that diversity.

NOTES

1. See V. Lossky, *The Mystical Theology of the Eastern Church*, James Clarke, 1957, ch. 8.
2. See J. C. Polkinghorne, *Science and Christian Belief/The Faith of a Physicist*, SPCK/Princeton University Press, 1994, ch. 10.
3. See summary and further references in J. C. Polkinghorne, *Scientists as Theologians*, SPCK, 1996, ch. 4.
4. See J. C. Polkinghorne, *Belief in God in an Age of Science*, Yale University Press, 1998, ch. 3.
5. See I. Prigogine and I. Stengers, *Order out of Chaos*, Heinemann, 1984; S. Kauffman, *At Home in the Universe*, Oxford University Press, 1995.
6. See Polkinghorne, *Belief in an Age of Science*, ch. 3.
7. See, for example, J. C. Polkinghorne, *Beyond Science*, Cambridge University Press, 1996, ch. 5.

6

FAITH IN THE HOLY SPIRIT

MICHAEL WELKER

The previous chapters 'Faith in God the Creator' and 'Faith in Christ' were written with an 'implicit pneumatology', with an implicit perspective on the Holy Spirit and its workings. There is no faith without the working of the Holy Spirit. But how can we grasp faith in the Holy Spirit? The implicit perspective on the Holy Spirit made itself felt among other things in the fact that I again and again spoke critically of 'abstract relations' to God and to Jesus Christ. To be sure, we can reach an individual, a personal relation to God through the revelation of God in Jesus Christ. Yet the relation to God is no abstract one-to-one relation. In personal relations to God the experience must not be lost that 'you surround me from all sides and hold your hand over me' (Psalm 139.5). The Lutheran and Reformed catechisms of the Reformation expressed this by the inconspicuous phrase that God does 'not only keep and rule *me*', but also *all* human beings, *all* other creatures, that God does not only speak to and has not only chosen '*all* Christianity', but also *me*. Thus the fact is made clear that 'relation to God' is not a purely private matter. It is not a relation which only grasps and shapes my inner self, which takes place only in my heart, only in my soul. A faith that does not want to owe itself to any other creature's witness, a faith that wants to remain absolutely isolated and speechless, is no Christian faith, no faith brought about by the Holy Spirit.

The Spirit – Filling the World, Yet Fleeing and Departing?

The Holy Spirit brings us into a relationship to God. But with this relation to God the Holy Spirit also renews inner-creaturely relations of life. The Holy Spirit is a vivifying and enlivening power. This does not at all mean – as some pneumatologies have maintained – that the Holy Spirit is causing absolutely everything and that this Spirit is in an equal way everywhere. Both abstract individualism and abstract universalism are fatal for the doctrine of the Holy Spirit as well as for theology in general. One of the few biblical statements which seem to represent an abstract universalism of the working of the Spirit is Wisdom 1.7: 'the Spirit of the Lord has filled the world, and that which holds all things together knows what is said'. The fact that this statement must not be understood in the sense of an abstract and unqualified omnipresence of the Spirit becomes quite clear two verses earlier in the same chapter, Wisdom 1.5: 'For the holy and disciplined Spirit will flee from deceit, and will rise and depart from foolish thoughts, and will be ashamed at the approach of unrighteousness.'

Entreating statements in the New Testament texts that human beings should not suppress the Holy Spirit, that they should not drive it away, that they should not extinguish it, that they should not afflict it[1] would be incomprehensible if we were to presuppose an abstract equal presence of the Spirit in every position of space and time in the universe. Structured life, life that corresponds to God's will, creaturely life is 'kept together' by the Holy Spirit. However, if God withdraws God's Spirit, creatures return to dust and perish (cf. Job 34.14f.; Psalm 104.29f.).

The Holy Spirit does not only keep creation together. The Spirit keeps and preserves creation precisely in delivering it again and again from powers hostile to God, in renewing and elevating it. Through the Holy Spirit God acts on and among creatures. God acts on them in that God chooses them for a life in the divine presence and enables them to such a life. The Apostles' Creed expresses this fact as follows, 'I believe in the Holy Spirit, the holy catholic Church, the communion of saints...'.

The 'Pouring' of the Spirit and the Ethos of Creative Difference

When we engage in conversation with the biblical traditions and ask what the nature of the community of saints is that is constituted by the Holy Spirit, then we come upon the figure of the 'pouring out of the Spirit', a figure that at first may seem strange. The Holy Spirit is 'poured' from heaven onto human beings and other creatures. Like rain from the sky that renews and refreshes a whole landscape and makes it flower and become fruitful in a communal life, thus God's Spirit renews complex conditions of life. The 'classical texts' among the witnesses to the workings of the Spirit are Joel 2 and the story of Pentecost, Acts 2.[2]

The promise that God will pour out his Spirit 'on all flesh' is explained by Joel in an emphasized differentiation, 'your sons and your daughters shall prophesy, and your old men shall dream dreams, and your young men shall see visions. Even upon the menservants and the maidservants in those days, I will pour out my spirit'. As in other statements about the workings of God's Spirit, the equal status of women and men is conspicuous in this promise. In patriarchal societies, this was sensational. Equally sensational for societies of classical antiquity is the equal status of old and young people. The marked equalization of old and young recipients of the Spirit does not agree with a social order in which only the old have 'a say'. Neither, of course, does it agree with a social order that idolizes the young and becomes hostile to the old. Finally, in this promise of the outpouring of the Spirit the equal status of so-called free persons and servants, both male and female, is expressly emphasized. And this in a slave-holder society, as most ancient societies were.[3] Constrictions and tensions that we still today deal with again and again are expressly stated. Tension between women and men, tension between old and young and tension between free and enslaved, between those who socially and politically are better off and worse off. The pouring out of the Spirit brings all these people into a new and living communal relationship before God and among each other.

We would not understand the promise in Joel correctly if we now thought, 'When the Spirit is at work, all human beings are granted the equal status of modern subjectivity.' For in this promise there is a particular granting of equal status. An equal status and a community are brought about in which creative differences are taken seriously. The promise does not say that all people will experience, think and say the same and will be equal in this abstract sense. Rather, it says, your sons *and* your daughters shall prophesy, your sons *and* your daughters shall disclose the knowledge of God with each other and for each other. Likewise, your old people *and* your young people shall for each other bear witness to God and God's presence. This, however, means that no longer just one group of people, the group which anyway has 'the say', shall determine the understanding of God and define faith. In the middle of creative differences God's vivacity is realized and taken seriously. Thus true freedom and an equality which puts differences to the test are promised.

Talk of the pouring out of the Spirit grasps a development that humankind has to a large degree still before it.

- We all, at least in most so-called Christian cultures, speak of the equality of all people, and yet countless people on this earth live below the level at which affluent countries keep their animals. They have to go hungry and often die miserably.
- We all speak of the equality of all people, and yet we have only laboriously started to give a voice in public to the feelings, experiences and knowledge of women in the same way as those of men. Only slowly do our cultures, our norms and our forms of life become consciously formed and shaped by women not only via the family, but also in many spheres of public life.
- We all speak of the equality of all people, and yet many of us have the greatest difficulty in entering into fruitful relations with people of other cultures and their world views and forms of life.

The transition from an abstract, typically modern understanding of equality, from an understanding of equality that is certainly full of merit but partly very untruthful, to an ethos of equality that is dynamic, sensitive to differences, that examines differences, differentiates creative from unjust differences and restructures them, this transition lies still before us. This transition which really perceives and takes seriously the forces of liberation through the Holy Spirit still lies to a large degree in our future.

What Happens at Pentecost?

Biblical statements about the Spirit and the pouring out of the Spirit take a vast step beyond 'liberal' communal forms which indeed intend an equality of all people, but in which only a particular group defines how the unity and equality are to be constituted. Even more than the promise in Joel does the Pentecost story urge us to take the *preserved differences* of the people and groups of people seriously who have been overcome by the pouring out of the Spirit. The account of Pentecost emphasizes: Here a new communality arises in the midst of preserved differences of culture, nation and language. In a plainly detailed, even lengthy, way different backgrounds of culture, nation and language are listed. Many groups of people are listed that do *not understand* each other. A long list is given which is to represent all people or which illumines the horizon of the Jewish world of those days: 'Parthians and Elamites, and those who live in Mesopotamia, Judea, Cappadocia, Pontus, and the province of Asia, Phrygia, and Pamphylia, Egypt ...' (cf. Acts 2). Here the world in all its differences of culture, nation and language is gathered. And all human beings, it says, understand 'the great deeds of God'. And with that long list the differences marked in the promise of Joel are also taken up. Differentiation of the many peoples, cultures and languages, differentiation of Jews and gentiles is thus drastically strengthened by the emphasized differentiation of men and women, young and old, maidservants and menservants. This is the Pentecostal community of the Spirit.

It is important to understand that the Pentecost account describes not just a case of glossolalia and an incomprehensibility in need of interpretation, but a wonderful comprehensibility.[4] The wonder of the pouring out of the Spirit lies in an improbable communal understanding in the midst of a difference of language, culture and social spheres. Without an elimination of the different languages, the different cultural affiliations and historical characteristics, a differentiated universal community is established. Where there is no natural presupposition of a successful understanding, the people brought together by the Spirit or seized by the Spirit or affected by the pouring out of the Spirit can together hear what is said about God's great 'deeds of power'. The Spirit of God thus does not only work through one people, or through one culture, or only through men or only through women or only through the old or only through the ruling class or only through the suppressed. Yet this understanding of a differentiated community established by the working of the Spirit meets with at least three questions.

General Difficulties in Understanding the Working of the Spirit

Question 1. *How do these statements relate to those of Paul that where God's Spirit is at work, where the risen Christ is present there is neither man nor woman, neither Jew nor Greek, neither slave nor free person and that we are all one in Christ, that through the Holy Spirit we all become one body?* Emphasis on the establishment of a differentiated community does not oppose the many statements about the unity of the Spirit or the unity of believers brought about by the Spirit. The Holy Spirit indeed establishes a unity of community, a unity in which faith, love and hope are vivid. It establishes a community in which righteousness, the protection of the weak and the knowledge of God and of truth are again and again sought for.[5] Under the working of the Holy Spirit the search for God and the love of God become concrete. God's Spirit constantly counteracts unjust differences. It transforms and relativizes natural and cultural differences which go along with injustice, lovelessness and hopelessness. However, this does not mean that the Holy Spirit simply eliminates differences. The unity of the Spirit is rather the unity and the interaction of the *different gifts of the Spirit*. The unity of Christ's body is the unity of the body with its different members. Paul again and again emphasizes this differentiated community of saints. To be sure, the whole body of Christ is ordered towards its Lord, towards the 'head', Jesus Christ himself. But in itself it is not monohierarchically organized. It is a body in which the differences of its members are crucial for living unity.

Paul expresses this fact very clearly when he says,

> by one Spirit we were all baptized into one body – Jews or Greeks, slaves or free – and all were made to drink of one Spirit. For the body does not consist of one member but of many. If the foot should say, 'Because I am not a hand, I do not belong to the body,' that would not make it any less a part of the body. And if the ear should say, 'Because I am not an eye, I do not belong to the body,' that would not make it any less a part of the body. If the whole body were an eye, where would be the hearing? If the whole body were an ear, where would be the sense of smell? But as it is, God arranged the organs in the body, each one of them, as he chose. (1 Corinthians 12.13ff.)

This not diffuse, but differentiated variety of the community brought about by the Spirit makes it quite clear to us that multi-perspectivity and a structured pluralism[6] is characteristic of faith[7] and of the contents of faith. In faith we deal again and again with witnesses: with a knowledge and a certainty *and* with knowledge of the limits of this knowledge and certainty. This complexity, however, makes people ask whether in the face of this multi-perspectivity and structured pluralism there will ever be something like a knowledge of faith and a certainty of faith.

Question 2. *Is this working of the Spirit as described above not absolutely chaotic; is the Holy Spirit not then a numinous entity?*
What is the nature of faith in the Holy Spirit; does it not lose all

knowledge and all certainty? With regard to the Holy Spirit this question finds an expression in scepticism over whether we can at all expect and strive for a knowing relation to the Holy Spirit. Retrospectively this question can relate to all knowledge of faith. Is it not presumptuous to make the attempt at all to relate to God in a way that is more than the speechless recognition of a numinous power? There have again and again been attempts to totally question the knowledge of faith with regard to the Holy Spirit and thus to define faith over against knowledge.[8] It has been said again and again: 'We do not know what we ask and search for when we ask and search for the Holy Spirit. But this is just right! The Holy Spirit is a numinous entity, an incomprehensible power. Whoever really wants to understand the Holy Spirit shows by this that he or she has not at all understood the Holy Spirit. The only thing we can know and say with certainty about the Spirit is that nothing certain can be known and said of it.'

This attitude has sometimes passed itself off as particularly pious. It has liked to refer to John 3.8, where it says, 'The wind blows where it chooses, and you hear the sound of it, but you do not know where it comes from or where it goes. So it is with everyone who is born of the Spirit.' The Spirit – a numinous entity not to be grasped, is that the answer to the riddle?

Like the wind, the Spirit is not to be grasped, not to be dominated, not to be determined. This statement is not wrong. It can claim for itself that in the biblical traditions the word for Spirit (*ruach* in the Old Testament and *pneuma* in the New Testament) can also refer to the wind. The Holy Spirit cannot be dominated and cannot be determined. This is certainly true. But it can as little be dominated and determined as God the creator. It can as little be dominated and determined as the crucified and risen Christ. It is simply nonsense to infer from the fact that we cannot dominate and determine God that we can speak of the creator and of Jesus Christ but not of the Holy Spirit. And it is equally inappropriate to infer from the fact that the Spirit cannot be dominated and determined that we cannot at all speak of God. 'Strive for the knowledge of God'; this is also true of the Holy Spirit. In the search for the knowledge of God we have to respect the vivacity and freedom of God. We have to keep in mind that we cannot dominate and determine God. We have to see clearly that we certainly miss God if we try to make God a categorically defined figure, if we so to speak fall from faith and make God a simple quantity of mere knowledge. But it is simply wrong to attribute an extra role to the Holy Spirit with regard to the problem that God cannot be known. Like the Holy Spirit, God's other forms of being are not at our disposal. And the Holy Spirit is no less open to the search for the knowledge of God than God the creator or God the Son.

But how should we understand the word of John, 'The wind blows where it chooses, and you hear the sound of it, but you do not know where it comes from or where it goes. So it is with everyone who is born of the Spirit' (John 3.8)? These clear questions can be answered clearly. We know the Spirit like the wind from its workings. From them we can know it. The Holy Spirit can be known from its workings, from the gifts and the fruits of the Spirit, and can be differentiated from other spirits. And with regard to the word of John, it emphasizes thoroughly the point that the Spirit is not at our disposal and cannot be dominated. A few other passages of Scripture put this similarly. But some hundred statements in the Bible emphasize that this is far from all that can be known and said about the Spirit. Only a handful of statements of the Scriptures speak of the Spirit not being at our disposal. More than 300 statements, however, say something definite about the Spirit. Instead of wreathing in mist the numerous statements about the definite workings of the Spirit by a handful of statements about the indeterminacy of the working of the Spirit it makes more sense to proceed the other way round and illumine the few statements about the Spirit not being at our disposal and its indeterminacy in the light of the many clear statements. The Holy Spirit can be known, in the middle of its freedom and despite the fact that we cannot dispose of it. It is this that we have to try to understand.

Question 3. *If it is right that the Holy Spirit works in the way of pouring out, and in the creation of a differentiated community, why does God work among people in such a complicated way?*
With this third question, the Apostles' Creed offers a key: 'I believe in the Holy Spirit ... the communion of saints, the forgiveness of sins ...'. To be sure, talk of the forgiveness of sins does not mean much to many people in our present-day culture. When sin is being talked of, they suspect they will be domineered over and ruled by people who assume superiority in moral knowledge, for example by religious and other functionaries. Sin – this word has become incomprehensible for most people.[9] When people who are on their second glass of whisky or their second piece of cream tart say, 'Now I am sinning,' or when they speak of

traffic and parking sins, then this helplessness becomes obvious. Even if they try they cannot understand what sin is. 'We are all little sinners, and so it has been always,' runs a song, sung at beer and wine festivals in Germany in a tipsy mood. And soon afterwards it says, 'We will all, all, all of us get into heaven because we are so good and well-behaved.' The talk of sin belongs to completely degenerate terms of piety. That is also the fault of the Christian Church and theology because it often grasped sin only as guilt, because it did not understand and did not teach to understand sin also as a power. We find this reduction of sin to guilt even in our confessions of sin.

Quite to the contrary, the biblical traditions have a clearer view. They see that sin certainly has something to do with guilt, but that it is more than guilt. Sin is also a power that enslaves people, that people cannot withdraw from. Sin as guilt and sin as a power which makes us ask, call and cry for God's righteousness – this differentiation should again become clearer in our confessions of sin. Then we would also understand again why we are in need of the power of the Holy Spirit if we want to be delivered from the power of sin.

Illuminating Early Witnesses of the Spirit's Working

We find the earliest testimonies to the action of God's Spirit in the Old Testament, in the book of Judges and in the first book of Samuel. The people of Israel or at least parts of the people find themselves in situations of danger in which no escape can be seen, in total hopelessness and in distress. Their annihilation is imminent or well under way. Israel was not without guilt that these situations arose, as is said repeatedly. It had turned away from its God. It had, as some texts read, done 'what was evil in the sight of the Lord'. In all these situations the people, the community, have given themselves over to resignation. They give up. They cry. They lament. They do not know what to do. The community is in despair. In all these situations the community thus does not want to fight any more. It is emphasized that it wants to evade a solution of the conflict by means of war. It is a situation that we could describe as follows: There is no sense in anything any more. We will perish. We are lost.

But then it says: And God's Spirit came upon such and such a person. This person succeeds in leading the people out of distress. These early charismatics overcome by God's Spirit are – according to the biblical witnesses – normal people, sometimes even a little ambiguous and not likeable. God's Spirit is experienced as an unexpected power not to be disposed of, and via such people it exercises its power that saves the community. The deliverance can be known. But nobody can say exactly why and how it happened. It is certainly not the merit of the community. Neither that of the noble personality of the charismatic. *God* has forgiven the evil that we did. *God* has again preserved and strengthened our community. *God* has torn us from destruction that seemed quite certain. In this situation it is said, *God's Spirit came down...*

In these early testimonies much remains unclear and ambiguous. The knowledge of faith grows, it increases – although not in a monolinear way – in the course of the biblical traditions and testimonies. Yet the earliest accounts of the liberating power of the Spirit already speak of a community that has been preserved through God's help. They speak of the forgiveness of sins. They speak of the restitution and the upbuilding of life that was close to death, that even seemed delivered to death. Thus they are not far from the Apostolic confession of faith: 'I believe in the Holy Spirit, the communion of saints, the forgiveness of sins, the resurrection of the flesh ...' At any rate, the accounts of the action of the Spirit in connection with so-called early charismatics are much closer to the Apostles' Creed than opinions and statements that the Spirit cannot be known.

The Power of Sin and the Power of the Spirit

In manifold ways do the biblical traditions represent the lostness of human beings who are caught by the power of sin. This power becomes most dramatically clear in Christ's cross. The cross reveals the sin of the world in its abysmal shape. It reveals that human sin is only partly, but not sufficiently grasped with the terms 'self-reference' and 'self-praise', that such terms even make it seem harmless. Jesus Christ is crucified in the name of religion, in the name of the Jewish and the Roman laws, in the name of leading politics and of the public opinion of his environment. In the cross the horrible triumph of the 'powers of the world' becomes obvious, which use God's good law to turn against God's presence and even to veil this very fact. In the cross it becomes evident that good law under the power of sin can become a complex mechanism of falsehood and deceit. In the cross it becomes obvious how people individually and communally distance themselves from God's presence, even use force to oppose God's presence and in all this are able to spread the *appearance* of righteousness, piety, political necessity and public consensus.

Christ's cross reveals the abyss of sin to us. It shows that our religion, our law, our politics, our morals, our public opinion can turn into weapons against God and God's presence. In such a process we can certainly work together with other people, other social classes, other cultures, other religions. We can do this in total naivety, without any consciousness that we have done something evil. Christ's cross again and again confronts us with this horrible possibility and reality. Against this deadly danger, even in the middle of this danger, God's Spirit realizes the justice intended by God, God's own justice.

In this situation it becomes inescapably clear that the pouring out of the Spirit is anything but a senseless or eccentric event. It is a healing necessity. Through the Spirit the diverse ways and forms in which people of diverse groups, times and cultures want to fulfil God's law become open and vulnerable to each other. Our search for justice, mercy and the knowledge of God – our search for the fulfilment of the law – is confronted with the search of other people for exactly this. Our religious, political, legal and moral achievements are questioned. Our self-righteousness, my own and our common one, is uncovered. This does not happen in order to compromise and expose human beings. This does not happen in order to lead them into confusion or into relativism. Human self-righteousness is uncovered in order to open human beings for the more perfect righteousness, for the greater mercy, for the clearer knowledge of God and of truth. God acts on them through the Holy Spirit. God takes them into his service through the Spirit.

Renewal and Uplifting by the Spirit

With God's Spirit human beings are given a wonderful power and force. It is not at their disposal, yet it can be clearly perceived. It questions them and yet builds them up. The Holy Spirit is a liberating, perfecting power, a power which again and again makes human beings consider the abyss of their helplessness and lostness. Without the Spirit, they would not be able to bear the message of Christ's cross. Without the Spirit, they would have to despair of the fact that the world can be tempted. Without the Spirit they would find themselves in a situation comparable to that of the despairing Israel in the book of Judges. However, even the most abysmal situation of human life is under the promise: God's Spirit has been poured out on you. On quite normal people who, as we mentioned, are sometimes even ambiguous and not likeable, like the early charismatics who were overcome by God's Spirit. God's Spirit is experienced as an unexpected power and one not at our disposal. Via such people it becomes a saving power.

But God's Spirit is not only a spirit of salvation. The creative God saves us by elevating us. The Spirit does not only again and again deliver us from our distress and entanglement. The Spirit takes God's creatures into a new life. They are given participation in the life of the risen Christ. They are deemed worthy to be members of his body. They are deemed worthy to be living building stones for God's temple. They become members of the 'new creation'. Through the Holy Spirit they become bearers of God's presence. Through the power of the liberating Spirit, not only is the situation under the power of sin revealed to poor and lost human beings, they are also liberated from this power. They are delivered from it by being presented with an immense dignity. They are granted community with Christ and participation in his life forces. They are given participation in the blessed and victorious overcoming of the resistance of human beings to God's presence and, along with it, in festive and peaceful community with each other.

Paul also describes this being given participation in God's power with the phrase that 'God's love has been poured into our hearts through the Holy Spirit' (Romans 5.5). At the same time he repeatedly describes a process of growth that is not quite easily understood, a process of growth of those who let themselves be grasped and shaped through the Spirit by God's love and by the love of God. *They engage in a relation to the living God which – in this relation – transforms them.* In love people are given participation in the identity and truth of God in such a way that these can gain shape and reality in them, in their body. Paul describes this fact as follows, namely that the 'love of Christ' actually 'urges' human beings to the perception that God's action invites us in Christ to gain participation in Christ and to be 'a new creation' (2 Corinthians 5.14–17). According to the letter to the Ephesians, loving persons receive a forever greater participation in God's power and essence, '*that you may be filled with all the fullness of God*' (Ephesians 3.19; cf. 17ff.). Here faith in the living God gains a clear shape: a knowledge that is also constantly confronted with its limits, a certainty which again and again is led beyond itself in the question for truth, because God's love wants to transform us so that we may be 'filled with the fullness of God'. The width and the wealth of faith can be perceived especially with regard to the Holy Spirit that brings us in touch with the creative God and with the presence of the resurrected Christ, in touch with the living God.

Comments: Four Pneumatological Points
JOHN POLKINGHORNE

As one would expect from the author of God the Spirit, *Michael Welker has many important and illuminating things to say about the person and work of the Holy Spirit. I wish to make four comments in response.*

The Spirit is indeed the spirit of relationality and so, because 'relation to God is not a purely private matter', we agree about the vital role of the Spirit-imparted life of the community. For both of us, the diversity of the gifts bestowed on individuals of that community, creating a differentiated equality among them, is a most significant way in which the Spirit works.

My second point relates to what is at first sight a most startling statement, when Michael says, 'This does not at all mean – as some pneumatologies have maintained – that the Holy Spirit is absolutely everywhere.' Why then does Psalm 139 ask 'Whither shall I go from thy Spirit? Or whither shall I flee from thy presence?' (v. 7). What are we then to make of so much Christian thinking that has wanted to speak of the divine omnipresence? I take this not to be a denial of these truths but a sharply phrased protest at the idea of 'an abstract omnipresence'. The latter would only be an appropriate concept for a force which, like gravity, was uniform in its action and not sensitive to context. In contrast, the personal presence of the Spirit is always perfectly attuned to the individuality of circumstance. Where the Spirit is denied and rejected, the divine presence will not overpower the opposition to itself, but it will remain, pleading the divine love even in the face of hostility. I tried to reflect something of this differentiated presence in the discussion that I grouped under my three headings.

My third point is to welcome Michael's concept of the 'pouring' of the Spirit as a necessary complement, perhaps antidote, to my emphasis on pneumatological hiddenness.

Finally, I would like to pick up the question of whether 'in the face of this multiperspectivity there will ever be something like a knowledge of faith and a certainty of faith'. It seems to me that if there is knowledge and certainty bestowed upon the Church, it is not in the form of a precise and detailed formulation, nor does it originate from a single identifiable human source but rather from the veiled and diffused working of the Spirit, whose gifts are distributed within the Christian community. It is important to me that the creeds, and conciliar conclusions such as the Chalcedonian definition, seem to delineate an area within which Christian discourse must be contained if it is to be validly related to the foundations of the faith, but not to specify a single exhaustive expression of faith and knowledge.

Reply: 'A Sharply Phrased Protest at the Idea of "An Abstract Omni-Presence"'

MICHAEL WELKER

I am very grateful for the revealing differentiation between the two forms: the power of the presence of the Holy Spirit and a force like gravity which is 'uniform in its action, and not sensitive to context'. Although the intrinsically 'personal' dimension of faith and the person-related working of God has been emphasized in most theologies, very often the poly-individuality and polyphony of circumstances was not expressed in the theological symbols, figures of thought and theories. I see both of us wrestling with this specific presence of the divine power and with a more adequate understanding of the texture of faith related to it. I see both of us deeply interested in comprehending this divine sensitivity to the individuality of circumstance without giving up a trust in the clarity of the divine working and its openness to comprehensibility.

I would like to understand the 'working of the Spirit from below' in emergent processes, that is in processes in which a complex set of relations is transformed not in a monohierarchical way, but in a divine working on many individual constellations and relations simultaneously. In emergent processes they are freed to interact with each other in surprisingly new ways and to bring forth complex new constellations. I agree that the power of many early Christian creeds lies in the ability 'to delineate an area' and to set boundaries within which Christian discourse and the search for truth can navigate and develop without losing its contents from view.

NOTES

1. 1 Thessalonians 5.19; Ephesians 4.30.
2. Cf. the following in detail: M. Welker, *God the Spirit*, trans. John Hoffmeyer, Fortress Press, 1994, esp. ch. 5; '"... And Also Upon the Menservants and the Maidservants in Those Days Will I Pour Out My Spirit": On Pluralism and the Promise of the Spirit', *Soundings* 78 (1995), pp. 49–67.
3. Illuminating on this issue, A. N. Whitehead, *Adventures of Ideas*, Free Press, 1967, pp. 14ff.
4. On this see my discussion with Frank Macchia, a Pentecostal theologian who wrote the most insightful and constructive critique of my book *God the Spirit*: 'Spirit Topics: Trinity, Personhood, Mystery and Tongues. A Response to Frank Macchia on *God the Spirit*', *Journal of Pentecostal Theology* 10 (1997), pp. 29–34.
5. On the 'fulfilment of the law', on the promotion of the good intentions of the law through the workings of the Spirit, see Welker, *God the Spirit*, pp. 18ff.; 109ff.; 125ff.; 253ff.
6. On the importance of differentiating structured pluralism and all sorts of vague 'plurality' see M. Welker, *Kirche im Pluralismus*, 2nd edn, Kaiser, 2000.
7. Dietrich Bonhoeffer has expressed this consequential insight in his *Letters From Prison*, esp. 29.5.1944.
8. Cf. Chapter 8.
9. Sigrid Brandt, Marjorie Suchocki and Michael Welker (eds), *Sünde. Ein unverständlich gewordenes Thema*, Neukirchener, 1997.

PART II

'FAITH SEEKING UNDERSTANDING' IN TRUTH-SEEKING COMMUNITIES AND AMONG INDIVIDUALS

7

OPENING WINDOWS ONTO REALITY

JOHN POLKINGHORNE

Human life is rich and many-layered. The same occasion may be experienced as a succession of physical events, as the setting of moral challenge and decision, as a value-laden experience of beauty, as an encounter with the sacred reality of God. For many worshippers, a church service can have all these dimensions and it could not adequately be described without taking them all into account. I suggest that we should welcome these multiple perspectives as affording us a many-eyed view of reality. This stance then commits me to a particular way of thinking about the complexity of human experience.

Experience

First, all levels present in that experience are to be taken seriously. Each of them opens up for us a window through which we may look out onto the world of which we are inhabitants. Some windows may be larger and better placed than others, so giving a more extensive view; some have distorting glass; some are clouded over and hard to peer through; all impose the limitations of their particular perspective. Yet all are looking out onto reality; all give us access from their specific point of view to the way things are. Second, I assert that reality to be one. It is by combining the different perspectives afforded by these many windows that we shall gain the most adequate understanding of who we are, what we can believe and what we can hope for.

These are large claims, which some would certainly contest. I shall not seek to substantiate them now in any detail, but I am content simply to state them in order to clarify the basis on which I approach the task of seeking truth and understanding. I am a passionate believer in the unity of knowledge, a belief that is underwritten for me by my trust in the one God who is the ground of all that is.

We have already looked through many windows in the course of our earlier discussions, as we sought perspectives on faith in the creator, in Christ, and in the Spirit. In this final personal contribution I want to add to that number and so to round out an account of my understanding of the nature and grounds for Christian belief. Of particular concern will be to seek to grasp the total significance of the created order, as much in its future as in its past and present.

Perspectives

First I shall open up a scientific window that I believe will afford us an important perspective whose significance can be expected to become yet clearer as twenty-first-century science develops. It looks onto

(1) *Spontaneously patterned complexity.* Scientists until now have largely pursued a policy of divide and rule, adopting the reductionist methodology of decomposing systems into their component parts as the way to produce situations of sufficient simplicity to be manageable. Slowly they are beginning the pursuit of a new science that reverses this trend. At present complexity theory is at the infant stage of having to rely on the study of computer simulations of moderately complex systems for its insights. No general treatment is yet known, but the specific examples that have been analysed begin to reveal intriguing features that indicate that there must be a deep underlying theory of considerable power and significance awaiting our discovery. The most striking behaviour found is the spontaneous generation of large-scale patterns of order of a wholly unexpected kind.

An example drawn from the work of Stuart Kauffman[1] illustrates the point. He studied a computer model whose structure would correspond to that of a large array of lightbulbs, each of which can be either on or off. Each bulb is correlated in its behaviour with two others somewhere in the array – if they are both on, then this bulb is more likely to be so also. The system is started off in some random configuration and then left to evolve according to the rules of the network. One might have supposed that it would simply flicker away haphazardly for ever. In fact, however, it soon settles down to a very regular behaviour. If there are

10,000 bulbs in the array, they will cycle through only about 100 different on/off patterns. Since the total number of such patterns in principle possible for the array is about 10^{3000}, this represents the generation of an astonishing degree of ordered behaviour.

Phenomena of this kind strongly suggest that where complex systems are concerned, their description requires not only the conventional account in terms of interactions between the parts, but also a complementary account relating to the patterned behaviour of the whole. In physical terms, this would correspond to working both with exchanges of energy between constituents and also with pattern-forming principles acting on the totality of the whole. The latter might be called principles of 'active information'.[2] One begins to see here the possibility of the revival of an old idea in modern dress: Aristotelian ideas of matter and form are being revived today under the rubric of energy and information. When we recall that Thomas Aquinas thought of the human soul as being the form of the body, we catch from this particular window a glimpse of a possibility that may be of great importance in a modern articulation of Christian eschatological hope. This is a point to which I shall return.

Perhaps matters will clarify if we add the perspectives from other windows. We need next to consider what comes into view if we look out through a range of windows labelled humane intuition. Two features seem particularly significant:

(2) *Finitude.* No aspect of the limitation of human nature is more obvious than our mortality. 'Golden lads and lasses must, as chimney sweepers, come to dust.' Yet we find within ourselves also aspirations that point beyond the curtailment of death, that refuse to grant the last word to human finitude. 'Death be not proud.' Human sad restlessness at the thought of the necessary incompleteness of any life lived in this world, human defiance of the apparent finality of death, are intuitions that we should take seriously into account. The more positively expressed side of this stance is seen through another window:

(3) *Hope.* Despite the strangeness, bitterness, incompleteness of this present life, human beings do not give way to despair. In the human heart there is something that responds to the conviction expressed so powerfully by the great fourteenth-century mystic Mother Julian of Norwich, that in the end 'all shall be well and all manner of thing shall be

well'. I think that this intuition of hope is an essential and significant aspect of what it is to be human. It is not just a survival technique for whistling in the dark to keep our spirits up, but it is an encounter with the reality within which we live.

The sociologist of religion Peter Berger draws our attention to this phenomenon of hope in his marvellous little book *A Rumour of Angels*.[3] Its concern is with everyday occurrences which, when we stop to think about what they actually mean, point us beyond the everyday to a more profound encounter with reality. Berger calls these happenings, 'signals of transcendence'. One of them is this: A child wakes in the night, frightened by a bad dream. A parent comforts the child, saying 'It's all right.' Berger asks us to think what is going on here. Is the parent uttering a loving lie about this world of cancer and concentration camps? Or is the parent conveying to the child a deep understanding of reality, an understanding that is an essential component in that child's growing into human maturity? Berger believes that it is the latter, and so do I. We possess a significant intuition that in the end all shall be well.

Eschatological Perspectives

When we put together the perspectives from the scientific and humane windows, what enhanced view do we obtain? There is a deep conviction of human hope, that we should take seriously. Yet the ground of that hope cannot lie in a mere evolutionary optimism, a belief that the unfolding of present process will lead to ultimate fulfilment, either individually or cosmically. If there is a ground for hope beyond the eventual futility of the universe's history, and beyond the certain mortality that is the individual human lot, then it lies outside the range of anything that science can discern or claim to be able to speak about. To put it bluntly, the only ground of true hope that there could be, within time and beyond it, lies in the everlasting faithfulness of the creator God.

This, of course, is exactly the point that Jesus made in his controversy with the Sadducees about whether there is a human destiny beyond death (Mark 12.18–27). He cut through their ingenious but shallow conundrum about the woman who had had seven brothers as her successive husbands, to point to the God of Abraham, of Isaac and of Jacob, 'the God not of the dead but of the living'. The point is clear enough. If the patriarchs mattered to God – and they certainly did – they matter to God for ever. The faithful God did not cast them aside at their deaths, as if discarding broken pots onto the rubbish heap of creation. We humans possess hope, not because we possess an intrinsic immortality or because life in our universe will go on for ever, but because we can commit ourselves in total trust into the hands of the God of everlasting love and mercy. I greatly love the words of the Charles Wesley hymn:

> Still let me prove thy perfect will,
> my acts of faith and love repeat:
> till death thine endless mercies seal,
> and make the sacrifice complete.

Death is the final act of acceptance and trust, given to us to perform in this world. Its acceptance can be our decisive moment of commitment to the God of Abraham, Isaac and Jacob, the God and Father of our Lord Jesus Christ.

Pursuing that theme further encourages us to look through a window which the Church provides for us. It is the window of

(4) *Sacramental experience*. Week by week the Christian Church throughout the world celebrates the Eucharist in obedience to its Lord's command to 'do this in remembrance of me' (Luke 22.19; 1 Corinthians 11.24–5). It is a profound spiritual experience with many layers of meaning,[4] in which the past event of the death of Christ is again made present and human sins are forgiven, and the gathered community participates in the future fulfilment of God's kingdom, celebrated in the presence of its risen Lord. This event in time that transcends the limits of the present moment is a fundamental experiential basis for the eschatological hope that is in the Christian believer. It grants an encounter with the reality of the triune God which is of the greatest importance and significance for the faithful.

Eschatological hope is not for humanity alone, for the implications of divine faithfulness go much wider than that. The creator must surely care, in appropriate ways, for the whole of creation. This vast universe is not there simply to be the backdrop for the human drama, taking place after an overture lasting 15 billion years. It is one of the messages to Job, spoken out of the whirlwind, that God has many purposes at work in the world. None of them will be frustrated. The universe itself must have a destiny beyond its death. There must be cosmic hope as well as human hope.

Eschatological hope, therefore, offers us a vision of immense scope. It is a vision that Christians must hold onto, and express to those around us, with as much clarity and conviction as we can attain. The Church must not lose its nerve about proclaiming the faithfulness of God and the final fulfilment of hope. At issue is the answer to an absolutely fundamental question: Does the universe make total sense or is it, in the end, 'a tale told by an idiot, full of sound and fury, signifying nothing'? My friend, and occasional atheist opponent, the distinguished theoretical physicist Steven Weinberg, takes the latter view. As a scientist, he is deeply impressed by the rational order of the universe, but from his 'horizontal', science-only perspective, it all ends in meaninglessness. As Weinberg notoriously said at the end of one of his books, he feels that the more he understands the universe, the more it seems to him to be pointless.[5] If there were only the scientific story to tell, only those scientific windows to look through, I would be inclined to agree with him. If the universe does have a point, if it really makes total sense – if it is truly a cosmos and not a chaos – that is because there is also a theological story to tell, of which we may become aware when we make use of the many other perspectives available to us onto reality.

We have seen that there is a yearning for a human destiny beyond death, but does such a hope really make sense? We must now address the issue of eschatological credibility. That question immediately raises the matter of how we are to understand the nature of the *human soul*.

A good deal of past discourse about a human destiny beyond death has been framed in Cartesian terms of the survival of a spiritual soul, which is detachable from the body and, in fact, survives the body's decay. It seems to me that today it is very hard to understand human nature in those classically dualist terms. Consideration of such matters as evolutionary history, linking us with less developed organisms, or the effects of drugs or brain damage on our mental states, points to humans being a much more integrated combination of the mental and the material than dualism expresses. Surely, we are psychosomatic unities, 'animated bodies rather than incarnated souls', to use a famous phrase. We can no longer think of ourselves as apprentice angels.

Such a conclusion would not have surprised the writers of the Hebrew Bible, who habitually thought of men and women as animated bodies. But then, if that is the right way to think, what has happened to the idea of the soul, surely in one way or another an indispensable element in Christian eschatological thinking? By looking out of the scientific window we have already caught sight of something that can help us. It is the concept of the soul as the information-bearing pattern, or 'form', of the body.

Whatever the soul may be, it is surely 'the real me', whatever it is that links the young schoolboy in the photograph with the ageing academic of today. That link is certainly not the mere matter of my body, for that is changing all the time, through wear and tear, eating and drinking. There is no basis for continuity to be found in the atoms of my body. Rather, the carrier of that continuity must surely be the dynamic, almost infinite, information-bearing pattern in which those atoms at any time are organized. That is the real me. The soul is the 'form', the pattern, of the body.

We have seen that this conclusion would have been congenial to both Aristotle and Thomas Aquinas. We should think that way as well, and if we do so it will help us to understand the nature of human eschatological hope of a destiny beyond death. That hope is not for a spiritual survival, for we are intrinsically embodied beings. But it is not the hope of a mere resuscitation either, the reassembly of the atoms of the body. It is the Christian hope of death and resurrection.

The pattern that is me will be dissolved at my death. Death is, therefore, a real end, but it is not the ultimate end, for only God is ultimate. It is a perfectly coherent belief that the pattern that is me will be remembered by God, held in the mind of the faithful creator, and that it will ultimately be reconstituted by God through the divine eschatological act of resurrection into a new environment. In other words, my soul will be preserved in the divine memory and then reembodied when I am raised to the everlasting life of the world to come.

That ultimate act of resurrection will not involve the matter of this present creation. Paul was right to say that 'flesh and blood cannot inherit the kingdom of God, nor does the perishable inherit the imperishable' (1 Corinthians 15.50). If it did, resurrection would only mean being made alive again in order to die again. Our destiny is something altogether more hopeful than that.

Two important questions then press upon us. The first is, What is this new 'matter' of the imperishable world to come? Putting it another way, using language that is also Pauline (2 Corinthians 5.17), how will God's 'new creation' relate to this old creation? I think that the answer is clear. The 'matter' of the new creation will be the redeemed matter of this perishing old creation. I have already said that I believe that the faithfulness of the creator implies that all creatures have an appropriate eschatological hope. Human hope and cosmic hope are inextricably intertwined.

But if that is so, a second question arises. If God can indeed bring about a world in which God 'will wipe away every tear from [our] eyes, and death shall be no more, neither shall there be mourning nor crying nor pain any more, for the former things have passed away' (Revelation 21.4), why did the creator not do so straight away? What was the point of this vale of tears and suffering, if the new creation can be so wonderful and joyful? Why did God bother with the old creation? It is a very serious question.

I think the answer lies in recognizing that, out of respect for the divinely granted integrity of creation, the creator acts through process and not through magic. The old creation of our present experience exists because of God's loving will that there should be something other than the divine self. Creation is allowed truly to be and to 'make itself', the latter phrase encapsulating the theological understanding of the nature of an evolutionary universe. Yet God's final intention is not that creation remains for ever separate, but that ultimately it shall share in the life of God, its creator. This freely embraced transition of creation from independence to union with the divine life is what we have called the eschatological redemption of the old creation into the new. In Christian understanding, this creaturely sharing in the divine life is brought about by the Cosmic Christ, who through his incarnation is the unique link between the life of creation and the life of God. The first chapter of the epistle to the Colossians presents us with the tremendous and hope-filled picture of the One through whom 'God was pleased to ... reconcile to himself all *things* [not just all people], whether on earth or in heaven, making peace by the blood of his cross' (Colossians 1.20).

God's purposes in creation are thus seen necessarily to be two-step, first the old and then the new. We live now in a world that contains sacraments; we shall live hereafter in a world that will be wholly sacramental, totally suffused by the expressed presence of the life of God. I do not believe in the panentheistic idea that the creation is within God as a present reality, but I do believe in panentheism as its eschatological destiny.

These ideas are deeply mysterious, exciting and hopeful. I believe that they are also coherent and credible. At their heart lies the concept of continuity in discontinuity. There must be sufficient newness, a sufficient degree of discontinuity, to ensure that the new creation is not merely the dismal tale of the eternal return of the old. Yet there must also be sufficient continuity to ensure that it is really Abraham, Isaac and Jacob who live that transformed life of the world to come. We can get some help by looking through a Christological window:

(5) *Encounters with the risen Christ.* It is Jesus who is raised, and his body still bears the marks of the passion. Yet he is not instantly recognizable. The appearance stories have the recurring theme of moments of initial puzzlement or misapprehension being followed by a moment of disclosure and recognition. Mary Magdalene mistakes the risen Jesus for the gardener, until he speaks her name and then she knows who it is. The couple on the road to Emmaus only realize to whom they have been speaking at the very moment when he disappears from their sight. Only the beloved disciple recognizes the figure standing on the shore in the light of early dawn as being the risen Lord, and when they come ashore the disciples cannot quite bring themselves to say 'Who are you?' In Matthew, the crowd on the Galilean hillside fall on their knees but, with great frankness, the writer tells us 'some doubted' (Matthew 28.17). There was sufficient discontinuity for recognition not to come easily. Jesus' glorified body is not just a restored entity in present spacetime, for it appears and disappears at his will. I see the appearance events as resulting from some kind of temporary intersection between the worlds of the old and new creations, meeting-places between the risen life of Christ, which is the seminal event giving birth to the new creation, and the continuing life of the disciples in the world of the old creation.

The empty tomb also tells us something of the connection between these two worlds. It implies that the Lord's risen body is his dead body transmuted and glorified, confirming the insight that the new creation springs from the redemption of the old creation. The empty tomb is of great theological significance, for it testifies that in Christ there is a destiny for matter as well as for humanity.

In modern scientific understanding, space, time and matter all belong together in an account of physical process. Einstein's general theory of relativity ties them together in a single package deal. I think that we may anticipate that this will also be the case in the new creation. In other words, there will also be 'time' as well as 'space' and 'matter' in the world to come. If human beings are intrinsically embodied, they are also intrinsically temporal. Our destiny is not to be outside time, in the unfathomable eternity of God, but inside the unfolding 'time' of the new creation. Spiritual fulfilment will not be given to us in some timeless instant of illumination, but through the unending exploration of the inexhaustible riches of the divine nature, accessible to us in that wholly sacramental world in which we shall everlastingly be 'in Christ'.

The creator who has acted, patiently and subtly, through the evolving process of this universe, is the redeemer who will act, patiently and subtly, within the unfolding process of the world of the life to come. Within that redemptive history there will be judgement (as we come in increasing measure to face reality and know ourselves as we actually are), purgation (as the accumulated dross of our lives is burnt away by the fire of the bright presence of God), healing (as we come to know how fully we are loved) and grace (as we become like Christ as we come to know him as he is (1 John 3.2)). These thoughts totally dispose of the criticism, sometimes heard within the Church as well as from outside it, that unending life would be unutterably boring. If we had simply to depend upon our own resources, that would certainly be so, but we shall be given a share in the infinite resources of God.

Christian faith and hope together form a great structure of integrated belief. Much is here that is mysterious as well as exciting, but the massive edifice of Trinitarian theology is not some building of baroque speculative construction, rather it is grounded in the foundations of the human experience of our interior spiritual lives and of the wonder of the universe in which we live, in our knowledge of the God who is both the creator of the world and the Father of our Lord Jesus Christ, and in the hidden work of the Spirit in our midst, drawing us on to participate in the ultimate fulfilment of the new creation.

NOTES
1. S. Kauffman, *At Home in the Universe*, Oxford University Press, 1995.
2. Cf. J. C. Polkinghorne, *Belief in God in an Age of Science*, Yale University Press, 1998, ch. 3.
3. P. Berger, *A Rumour of Angels*, Penguin, 1970.
4. See, M. Welker, *What Happens in Holy Communion?*, trans. John Hoffmeyer, Eerdmans and SPCK, 2000.
5. S. Weinberg, *The First Three Minutes*, Andre Deutsch, 1977, p. 149.

8

SPRINGING CULTURAL TRAPS

MICHAEL WELKER

Most of the definitions and theories of culture seem to agree explicitly or implicitly on the fact that cultures serve the communication of human beings via memories and expectations. With the help of our culture we develop astounding abilities to connect and disconnect, to share and to differentiate our memories and our expectations. In our memories and imaginations we anticipate, reproduce and reconstruct what others remember, anticipate and expect. Moving in the realms of memory and imagination we attune our emotions, thoughts and practices in very powerful ways. To achieve this we do not even have to talk to each other, to see each other and to touch each other all the time. We can, so to speak, manage most of our communication by flying above physical reality and concrete person-to-person encounters, with only occasionally illustrative landings. The complex entity 'culture', which one sociologist called the 'brain of society', makes this possible.

Part of the particular power of our current cultures is that they provide high degrees of secure common memories and expectations, although they can host very different sets of values and virtues. We can put ourselves into others' shoes although in fact we do not share exactly the same hierarchy of values and virtues. This ability is greatly enhanced and cultivated in late modern pluralistic societies and cultures. Different 'societal systems', as sociologists say, operate with different symbol-systems and rationalities: law, politics, the market, the sciences, education, the arts, religion – they do not follow one common code. Moreover, most of these systems or spheres are highly differentiated in themselves; for instance the sciences and the humanities, the differentiated system of the markets, the highly patterned world of the media and of infotainment, and the oecumene of the Christian churches and the orbit of the religions. We live in a complex world that does not exhibit a one-hierarchy order, but rather a multi-hierarchical texture. Our cultures enable us to navigate in this world with some trust and some success.

At a closer look, however, the powers of our cultures to reach an attunement or at least clear differentiation of shared memories and expectations appear limited. The relation of theology and science seems to reveal some of these limits. The interesting question now is whether these limits are grounded in a reality 'out there' – or whether these limits are due to the texture of our culture. Are we even trapped by our culture, blinded, led into systemic distortions? We certainly know that our cultures are no innocent entities. To be sure, on a *second-order* level of thinking, we rightly give high praise to a culture as such. Most people associate culture with 'goodness', and the association of 'goodness' with 'morals', 'the ethos' and, for many, with 'religion' also holds true. Although human beings cannot live without cultures and morals and at least latent forms of religion, on a *first-order* level all these indispensable forms of ordering, shaping and freeing human life can become partially or totally corrupted. Examples are racist, fascist and Stalinist cultures, and cultures with an ecological brutality that is simply unbelievable. Is the seemingly widening gap or even split between science and theology in our cultures a sign of such a distortion, a minor distortion at least? Are we somehow trapped by our culture?

The following contribution draws attention to the fact that in our current culture there are indeed several traps that alienate common sense, religious experience and scientific thinking. It shows how the discourse between scientists and theologians on specific topics led to the discovery of such powerful traps. It concentrates on two traps in particular that have blocked an understanding of time and eternity and of a living God. The whole chapter thus provides some theoretical background to the previous chapters on Christian faith in the Triune God.

The Turn Toward Theological Topics in the Discourse Between Science and Theology

Time and again we have been told that modernity brought about a continually widening gap between the natural sciences and theology. To be sure, modern common sense experienced a steadily growing distance to the world of the mathematized sciences on the one hand and to the sphere of the world religions on the other hand. Many people hoped to find a way out of this fix by allocating religion to the 'strange world of the past' and the sciences to the equally 'strange world of the future'. At the same time they profited both from religion's powers to shape aesthetics, morals and people's mentalities, and from the predictabilities and technological benefits science brought with it. Somehow the powers of the so-called past world and of the so-called future world both came together in the present.

The more or less lazy, if comfortable, ignorance of modern common sense with regard to the natural sciences and religion (respectively theology) is not the only problem. Even scholars with great academic gifts seem to have enormous difficulties in bridging the gap. The complexities of an adequate scholarly treatment of religious topics and the complexities of an adequate scholarly treatment of natural-scientific topics are so demanding in themselves and they seem so incompatible with each other, that only very few human beings are able to seriously and actively join in the academic discourse in both realms. A human life seems not long enough and a human brain seems not potent enough to become truly familiar with both worlds. The times of the 'universal geniuses' are long gone, we are told. What priests and healers in some remote parts of our planet seem to be able to embrace in the life-worlds of their tribes, namely the whole world, seems absolutely impossible in a world which witnesses or at least believes in its market-, media- and technology-driven 'globalization'.

Modern science and modern theology have, of course, not simply submitted to resignation in the face of this development. They have not simply given up belief in one world, one reality, the unity of knowledge, the unity of truth. Many modern scientists became, as Carl Friedrich von Weizsäcker once put it, 'agnostic, but open' toward religion. To be sure, there are those who reacted quite aggressively to religion and theology, assigning it to the realms of other-worldliness, of hyper- and virtual reality, of mere personal feeling and a mere certainty that is not able to sustain truth-claims. Others honoured this so-called realm of meaning or the so-called existential realm. And not a few theologians specialized in the realms of meaning and existence, often moving into all sorts of moralism, lay therapy and entertainment. The more academically oriented theologians and scientists, however, resisted this development by claiming that at least the history of the past, the interest in past worlds and past truth-claims should keep theology in the academic orbit.

But this type of resistance concerned with history also had its price. The good news always seemed to be yesterday's news. Academic theology became obsessed with the history of religion and – with itself, its own history. Doing good jobs in interpreting and reinterpreting past worlds and its own classics, academic theology only seldom risked an analytical theological view of the societal and cultural reality of today. Only in times of trial and trouble did a truly systematic theology come alive. Those, however, who did risk addressing issues of the present and the future seemed to move toward the boundaries of their academic disciplines or even across the border. Very often they became active speakers for specific causes. In such cases, theologians who for instance were ecologically concerned came together with scientists who were ecologically concerned. But the commonality in the moral agenda did not – or at least did not yet – provide a commonality that could be transported back into the academic orbit and stimulate interdisciplinary work. In most cases a moral commonality was gained at the cost of an estrangement from the academic environment.

The final approach with which some academic theologians tried to react against the widening gap between theology and science was a move toward radical abstraction or toward a transcendentalization of all religious topics. Speaking of God just as 'the ultimate point of reference', or of faith as a trusting relation to the other side of my inner self-reference, they tried to offer ultimate forms that no reasonable person could resist accepting. The high price of these offers of theology and religion 'in a nutshell' was finally the self-secularization and self-banalization of theological discourse. While some scientists accepted this needle-point theology as an attempt toward academic honesty, most of them chose to find it simply boring. For a growing number of people who do no longer feel at home with the metaphysics of the ultimate point or with post-Cartesian subjectivity, these theological offerings are nothing but declarations of bankruptcy: the lust to control everything by one construct or one thought alone. A naive confusion of the unity of reality and truth with one simple thought or idea – if this is all theology has to offer, we had better get rid of this pretentious enterprise. In the midst of all these not very inviting and convincing general moves to set things straight again, we have, however, seen more promising and more illuminating moves between science and theology.

In 1993 the Center of Theological Inquiry in Princeton under its former director Daniel Hardy sponsored a four-year consultation in which a highly interdisciplinary group (including the fields of cosmology, physics, chemistry, biology, environmental studies, philosophy, religious studies and theology) moved

- from an exchange over different disciplinary and individual approaches to the dialogue between science and theology,
- to the discussion of religious topics of common interest and, finally,
- to a progressive specification of common theological and epistemological grounds of discourse.

In the second year the notion of *divine activity* was selected and discussed in a multitude of perspectives. In the third year the notion of the *temporality of God's action in the world* was chosen in order to gain more specificity. In its last year the consultation centred on the two topics: *eternity and temporality* and *eternity and contingency* in God's acting in the world.

This persistent drive towards a specifically theological topic and interface of the dialogue was new, and exciting for many of us. Up to this time I had witnessed several constellations of dialogue which were more or less far away from the interest in a genuinely *theological* focus. I had had the chance to participate in forms of discourse which worked on historical questions concerning the relation of science and theology, on ethical concerns, on general methodological reflections or on the endeavour to test a certain philosophy (particularly the philosophy of Alfred North Whitehead) as a potential interface for the dialogue. With one exception (in a discourse in the field of sociobiology) the inner complexity of theological topics and forms of thought had not had a chance to have an impact on the discourse or to get shaped by the discourse. It was rather a religiously shaped common sense, sometimes enlightened by popularized philosophical modes of thought, which was the real partner of the dialogue. The Princeton discourse was different: there was an eagerness on the part of many scientists to engage in some theological complexity. And there was some willingness on the theological side not to overrule scientific insights into reality by metaphysical presuppositions. This caused a new and exciting climate of discourse.[i]

Discovering and Springing Cultural Traps

The discovery that an interdisciplinary discourse on a genuinely theological topic can maintain a critical and nuanced realism provided excitement in our group. It became clear that both science and theology have to deal with realities seen and unseen and that they have different standards of intelligibility that can be explored and explained across the boundaries of the disciplines. The unseen reality with which theology deals is not a soft element that allows for all sorts of vague guesses and a speculative 'anything goes'. We do have *standards of intelligibility* in both disciplines to disclose the realm of the unseen. And one of the most exciting tasks of the science and theology discourse is to discover, to disclose and to reshape these standards in conversation on a specific topic. This might indeed lead to a clear differentiation of their tasks. A subtle, critical and self-critical adjustment of this differentiation and difference needs to be aware of several traps that mutually reinforce each other. It enabled us to question a whole set of mostly latent presuppositions that had governed and restricted much of our own previous thinking and certainly also the thinking of other theories we used to work with. In the following I should like to give an account of these discoveries embedded in our progress. I will name and describe as cultural traps six complex restrictions which reinforce each other.

The *first trap* can be called the *modernist trap*. This is the illusion that we can and must reach a universal perspective that can integrate all the different cultural spheres or disciplines with a simple epistemic move. For the science and theology discourse that meant the opinion: We just have to establish a methodological, metaphysical or transcendental level, we have to reach a level of a meta-discourse in order to bridge the gap between both of them. Without denying the value and importance of such strivings, we should become aware that this attempt easily loses contact with both sides, playing in a realm of a philosophical or quasi-philosophical theory which develops icons and ideals of science and theology accessible to common sense, but does not do justice to either one of them. Instead of encountering and enduring the differences and looking for both continuities and discontinuities between their realms of experience, it tends to smooth and to idealize both commonalities and differences.

The *second trap* easily goes together with the first, but is not identical with it. I would like to name it the *trap of reductionism*. This trap comes as a signal or as a conviction that we should, or even have to, minimize or avoid content in order to bridge the gap between science and theology. This reductionism can happen on either side. There have been many discourses in which science entered with all its complexity and glory, while theology only came up with such reductionist and boring ideas as the 'ultimate point of reference' or a transcendental inwardness named 'faith', or a realm of the numinous that reduces us to silence. But we have also, although more rarely, experienced the other reductionism, where science was ciphered as a representative of a certain concept of nature, a specific understanding of reality or of 'the law'. These concepts of 'nature', 'reality' or 'the law' happened to fit into a certain theology. Science's own complexity was taken away. It was simply reduced to a sparring partner of a specific theology.

The first two traps can reinforce each other, adding plausibility to each other, but creating systematic and systemic distortions. Although we certainly cannot avoid employing selection and the reduction of complexity, and although we have to work with typifying modes of thought and leading abstractions, a radical reductionism leads to a self-banalization that is not helpful at all for the science and theology discourse.

The *third trap* could be called the *dualistic world view trap*. This trap serves as a complementary companion for the two previous traps. Each of these or both can recommend themselves as great aids in escaping from the dualistic turmoil. We certainly cannot and should not avoid dualities, differences, contrasts and even conflicts in our life and thinking. But we should not freeze them into a great dualism. Rather, we have to face many types of difference: creative differences, form-giving differences, differences that are hard to bear and differences that are distortive and even demonic. The complex relation between science and theology can turn out as a fruitful one as long as we remain sensitive to this spectrum of differences and avoid the great frozen dualisms.

We have to become aware that science in itself is highly differentiated, and that the differentiations and differences between the theologies in one religion are considerable, let alone the differences between theologies of different religions. So we have to work with provisional, tentative, topic-centred differentiations and dualities. We have to avoid the danger of turning stale in frozen procedures which are overly generalized and lose touch with the specific topic. In such situations we are easily led from one trap to the next.

First a situation with no way out is created by fixing absolute dichotomies, and then we are lured into reductionism or into the modernist trap by the respective promise that it offers a solution to get out of this mess. Only when we discover and disable the trap of the great frozen dualisms can we see that the two sides belong to different *truth-seeking* communities, with different primary topical fields and certainly different modes and methods.[2] We all belong to truth-seeking communities which have to explore commonalities, analogies and differences in their procedures. We cannot do this once and for all, but instead must do it with a clear awareness of the topics at issue and of the contexts of the partners in discourse.

The *fourth trap* I would like to describe can be closely related to the dualistic world view trap. It can be called the *cliché trap*. The cliché trap picks up some characteristics of either theology or science or both of them and overgeneralizes and overstates them. For instance, science deals with facts – theology deals with meanings or mere fictions. When such a trap combines two clichés in a popular dualism, it is particularly difficult to spring. Even if one felt that there was only *some* truth in the characterization of the one side, there was still the other side to be respected. And the other side was all too often protected by what I should like to call the Frederick-the-Great syndrome.

Frederick the Great, king of Prussia in Germany, loved to play and compose music, and he loved to write poems. It is said that the poets used to say, 'His poetry is awkward, but he is a great musician!' and the musicians are reported to have said, 'His music is hard to bear, but his poems are outstanding!' The Frederick-the-Great syndrome easily casts a shadow on any kind of interdisciplinary work, and presents a real danger to interdisciplinary agendas. But it can also be used as a denunciation ready at hand. Moreover the Frederick-the-Great syndrome can stabilize distortive dualistic clichés, such as the following:

science deals with facts – theology deals with meaning;
science deals with objectivity – theology deals with individual feeling.

When theologians and scientists come upon such dualities, they may each want to protest against the presentation of their own side. But then, there is the other side to be considered with its somehow, somewhat plausible contrast, and this may in the end make many swallow their initial dissatisfaction.

The *fifth* and *sixth traps* are cultural traps that block a realistic and sound understanding of time and eternity and an understanding of the living God's relation to eternity. I should like to discuss these traps in more detail. The former is constituted by false generalizations of time and false oppositions of time and eternity. The latter is constituted by a theism which cannot imagine and think the living Triune God and thus has to confuse eternity with what Hegel called 'bad infinity'.

A Critique of the Abstract Opposition of Time and Eternity

In the twentieth century the efforts to overcome the abstract opposition of God and time, of eternity and temporality and to conceive the connection of God's eternity and God's temporality belonged to the great projects of theology and the humanities. This endeavour aimed at ending a long and significant tradition. Influenced above all by Plato, classic theologians from Augustine to Schleiermacher had maintained that God was *beyond time*, and that whereas creation was essentially temporal, God was essentially timeless. In the nineteenth and twentieth centuries, philosophers like Hegel and Whitehead drew attention to the various problems connected with this assertion. In the twentieth century, such diverse theological schools as dialectical theology and process theology agreed in their efforts to free God and the theological concept of eternity 'from the Babylonian captivity of their abstract opposition to temporality'.[3]

This, however, is more easily attempted than achieved. We cannot maintain that so far theology and the 'neo-classical metaphysics' of process thought have reached new consolidated positions.[4] 'Among the most puzzling, and the most pressing, of general questions about God are those concerned with how (God) is to be understood to relate to time. It is clear that there must be an *eternal* pole to the divine nature. God's steadfast love can't be subject to fluctuation if God is worthy of being called divine. Emphasis on this alone would lead us to a static picture of God, but could that be true if the nature of love is relatedness and that to which God relates, namely God's creation, is itself subject to radical change?'[5] This description of the problem makes it clear that to renounce a conception of God's eternity cannot be the answer to the problem.

The biblical traditions conflict with an abstract opposition of God and time, of God's eternity and temporality, when they speak of God's life or God's knowledge, of God's deciding or intending action and also of God's revelation in the earthly, crucified and resurrected Jesus Christ. All such statements challenge us to give up the 'Babylonian captivity' of our thinking about God, to give up the abstract opposition of God's eternity and temporality. After what we have said, a way out of this dilemma, however, can only be offered by a convincing concept of God's eternity which permits us both to differentiate eternity from creaturely temporality and to relate eternity to creaturely temporality.

The great Swiss theologian Karl Barth made a suggestion to solve the problem by postulating a metaphysical doubling of the past–present–future structure of time, by calling this 'super-time' ('pre-temporality, trans-temporality, post-temporality') God's 'eternity' and by identifying it with God. 'Pre-temporality, trans-temporality, and post-temporality are at the same time God's eternity and thus the living God himself.'[6] This starting-point, however, can only satisfy those who are ready to accept a speculative top-down construction which offers a paradoxical constellation, namely God's identification with and God's opposition to the totalized 'almighty time' (Hegel). On the one hand, Barth, in offering a past–present–future structure, identifies God and eternity with an infinite self-surpassing of time; on the other hand, he opposes God and eternity to totalized time by a pre-, trans- and post-rhetoric. Thus he offers a paradoxical metaphysical construct. Those who do not like to start with vague notions of surpassing, pretended concepts of totality and paradoxes have to look for another solution.

The alternative, however, which in the following we take up and try to develop further, not only makes it necessary to call into question the abstract opposition of God and eternity over against time and temporality. It also forces us to call into question the **totalization and unification** of time, and thus to end a second famous tradition of thought. Since Aristotle and Augustine, 'time' has been regarded as the universal condition of objective nature or as the universal form of human perception. Although in the twentieth century the power of clocks and watches and calendars rather increased, scientific observations and discussions in the past decades have called into question this totalizing and unifying view of time.

Ingolf Dalferth states convincingly: 'Our explanations of time are proof that we do not only thematize time in different approaches to the same phenomenon, but, in fact, have our eye on different phenomena: the metric time of physics, the life rhythms of biology, psychology's systems of experiencing time, the processes of perception of our everyday consciousness, the symbolic order systems of sociology, the causal structures of procedure and *a priori* forms of perception in philosophy, the historical chronologies of historical disciplines, the differential relations between time and eternity in theology – they all, under the catchword "time", thematize problems whose diversity makes clear above all "that 'time' is no fixed idea without exception and unambiguous definiteness" . . . '[7]

Independently of the question (which still needs clarification) whether these phenomena and fields of phenomena have a common basic structure (e.g. J. T. E. McTaggart's B-series, that is the structures of a real 'earlier' or 'later' of events[8]), the start from a plurality of times and conceptions of times opens up new chances of a genuinely theological handling of the problem with which we began; however, it confronts us with new difficulties as well. The new chances lie in the fact that starting from a plurality of times – a procedure open to a bottom-up approach – is in principle more appropriate to subtle everyday experience on the one side and to the biblical traditions on the other than starting from the imputation of the one time. However, at the same time, as James Barr has shown, the different conceptions of time in different experiential contexts raise great problems of translation from one into the other and of fine-tuning among each other.[9] 'If we have time' only as a vehicle of 'orientation that can be formed in various ways and is historically changeable', as Norbert Elias formulated,[10] this vehicle of orientation that threatens to become blurred in an immense abundance of phenomena, ironically leads to its own form of misleading abstraction. In my opinion, however, the insecurity caused by the observation of a plurality of times can be overcome, if – as Ingolf Dalferth has suggested[11] – the meaning and function of the 'ontological and eschatological differences of times' is taken into account. The meaning and function of the religious differentiations of 'temporality and eternity' must be observed and more closely examined in connection with the differentiation of 'the old times' and 'the new times', the old and the new aeon. The religious difference between the old and the new time, the old and the new aeon enables us to grasp and to differentiate complex orders of the connections of the times.

In this enterprise, however, 'eternity' or 'the new time' must not again be perceived as concepts of mere abstract totality or as a basis for the development of abstract totalizing perspectives on 'all times'. Unfortunately, even Dalferth seems to suggest that.[12] Rather, we need to consider more closely *God's activity*, God's formative powers with regard to the times in order to understand from this starting-point 'eternity' and 'the new time' in difference and in relation to merely creaturely times or 'the old time'.

God's Coordination of Times:
The Creativity of the Triune God

The biblical traditions speak of a plurality of times 'created' by God: times of the day, times of the year or seasons, individual times of life, social times of life, times of festivity, etc. These times occasion a multiplicity of orders and orientations, and coordination of various processes of life which partly agree with each other, but partly do not. Rhythms of life structured by the times of the day and seasonal plannings for harvesting and for supplying food may be well adapted to the expected development of the vegetation. But individual and social structures of times of life – such as birth, love, illness, ageing, death, difficult developments – interfere with such attunements in ways that are by no means always fruitful and life-promoting. In some areas of space and time biographies and communal histories are blessed by a wonderful rhythmic coordination of climate and natural conditions, in others they are hindered in their development or even become destroyed.

If we intend to focus on this net of interferences constituted by the various times, it becomes clear that there is a constant necessity to connect and coordinate the various times. Continuities, simultaneities and seasonabilities need to be ensured, made possible and realized in their coordination.

This coordination can only in a very limited way be guaranteed and looked after by human beings alone. A life-promoting coordination of creaturely times is improbable and continually jeopardized. Therefore a constant search for knowledge of the power and the potentials of the 'fullness of times' – sometimes symbolized by 'the heavens' – is necessary to further the relations of fruitful, good, ordered and at the same time creative connections of the most heterogeneous fields and phenomena of time. The creation account in Genesis 1 speaks of divine and creaturely attunements of cosmological, biological and cultural realms of phenomena and temporal rhythms.[13] In order to be able to cooperate in this coordination, human beings must be enabled to ask God – according to Genesis via the cult – in suitable ways for the creative coordination of times. For even where human beings themselves are not able to guarantee the interferences of times, these interferences do not happen without them and without their co-activities nor without the co-activities of other creatures. In this process, human beings (and possibly also other creatures) do have numerous possibilities to misunderstand

and hinder God's intentions. Under the condition of active and passive opposition by human beings God's revelation occurs through God's creative coordination of times.

This does by no means imply – as a theological misjudgement says, which one constantly meets with – that God is automatically active and present in *each and every* place of space and time! God, by turning away God's face, by lowering or veiling it, as the biblical texts say, can rather leave times to the destructive dynamics of creaturely misdevelopment. This by no means implies that God *has to* leave certain realms of creaturely life and thus certain times to their own destructive power.[14] All times are *coram deo*, but God is not automatically active and present in all of them. In order to understand and express this we should grasp God's relation to time as a living aggregation or relation of times which includes their *fullness, but not their totality*. In my opinion, this is exactly what is aimed at by the biblical concepts of 'eternity' and the critical differentiation of 'the old aeon' and 'the new aeon'. The expression 'eternity' is on the one hand used for extremely distant and removed times in the past and in the future ('from eternity to eternity...'). On the other hand, it is used for the source and the resources of times which in the coordination of times make possible *unfathomable duration and permanence*. Since not all the times and all the coordinations of times correspond to God's will and God's intentions, and will perhaps not even correspond to them in any possible future, and since many coordinations of times are mediated by creatures and thus do not *automatically* correspond to God's good will, it would be wrong to understand God's eternity as *a priori* equally related to *all* times.

In any case, there are times that are 'old', that will disappear or that are destined to vanish. There are times that work against God's actions and God's self-revelation in destructive and self-destructive ways and that therefore can at best further God's good plans with God's creation *in unexplainable and unimaginable ways*. But how can we know God's intentions with regard to structured finitude? How can we understand and explain the workings of the eternal God under the conditions of temporal finitude? I think that Trinitarian theology starts out here and helps us to perceive the divine and the divine activity in the midst of finitude and at the same time to eliminate the idols and ideologies which mix with this perception. In the Trinitarian differentiation we track God's creative, revealing and life-sustaining identity and power in the cooperation of God's modes of being or the so-called 'persons' of the Trinity who each have *traits* of eternity and yet only *together* constitute God's fullness, pleroma, doxa and eternal life.[15]

The Triune God and Eternal Life

In the Priestly creation account it is remarkable that in the process of creation cosmological, biological and cultural rhythms and times are attuned to each other. These times, all of them times 'below heaven', which quite decisively are determined by the orbits of the heavenly bodies, are once more differentiated from God's time, from the famous 'seven days' of the Priestly creation account.[16] Even here it becomes clear that 'creation' is not simply the arrangement of various times which can be measured by chronometers or other scientific achievements: in that the earth's own activity, human beings' interests in self-reproduction and the problem of domination and preservation of fellow-creatures are integrated into the process of creation, factors enter this process which make simple structures of preserving and securing 'the eternal recourse of the same' appear insufficient from the point of view of creation theology.

In spite of this the prevalent time structure of creation in the sense of the first article of faith seems to me to be stamped by this attunement of cosmological, biological and human-cultural times in the sense of preservation and the guarantee of rhythms and continuity, reciprocity and security of expectations. If in the thought of God 'the creator' we abstract from the second and third articles of faith (which really is theologically inadmissible), we have before us Gordon Kaufman's vague concept of the cosmic planner on a grand scale. The so-called 'natural experience of God', which is not to be equalled with 'natural theology', as Wolfhart Pannenberg has shown,[17] is frequently directed towards this God. This 'natural experience of God' is vague, as Calvin clearly states in his *Institutes* I.3, or, as he puts it more pointedly, it is 'vain and fleeing'. Yet it is very powerful.[18]

I am a little at a loss with regard to an appropriate term for a synthesizing form of time, expressed in connection with and attunement to cosmological, biological and cultural times, that allows for rhythm and continuity. With openness to a better phrasing, I would like to suggest that we speak of a *connection of times that can be universally measured*. Abstract theism with its strong interest to apply all sorts of abstract 'omni'-quantors to the divine obviously centred on this understanding of temporality. Abstracting from the other two articles of faith and the temporality expressed by them, this notion of God and time destroys not only Trinitarian thought but also all notions of a living God. It leads to a confusion of eternity and infinity, or, as Hegel termed it, 'bad infinity' (*schlechte Unendlichkeit*). In connection with the other articles of faith, however, this notion allows, as we shall see, for an understanding of the divine in a connection of three rich 'wreaths of metaphors' which we find in the biblical traditions.

With regard to the second 'Person' or way of being of the Trinity, a form of time becomes central which we could term the **complex of historical times**. These temporal forms centre on specific events and complexes of events which shape and mark the course of a multitude of other events in particular ways. Its structure is irreversibility and that of past–present–future. For Christians, this time is decisively determined by the appearance and activity of Jesus of Nazareth, by the radiance of Jesus' post-Easterly life, and by the effects of this on church and world history. Old Testament traditions, however, emphasize that God's revelation in the Messiah is not the only way of God's self-historicization.

God's creative 'eternity' makes itself known in the connection and mutual penetration of universally metricizable and reversible times and historical, biographical, irreversible times.[19] Even if at times we tend to attribute the great constancies and rhythms to the true creator and keeper of 'heaven and earth', we must not overlook the fact that God's truly creative and formative power cannot at all be conceived without the activity of the second mode of being of the triune God. If we abstract from the second and third modes of being, we do not overcome the region of ambiguous statements, e.g. that God lets the sun shine upon good and bad people alike. But: *Opera trinitatis ad extra indivisa sunt!* It is only in the connection of universally metricizable and reversible times, and historical, irreversible times which differentiate past, present and future, that the creator and keeper of the universe acts upon God's creatures in a way called 'creative', 'ruling' and 'guiding'. And it is only in this **perichoresis of times** that the resurrected and exalted Christ acts as *logos* and mediator of creation, as the power of the living God in which all the promises are included.

The form of time of the third article is to be differentiated from both these forms of time, but it is irrevocably connected with them and stands in a differentiated unity with them. With regard to the metaphor of the 'pouring out of the Spirit' we can clarify this form of time which already lies at the basis of the coordinations of each, the universally metricizable and reversible times, and historical, irreversible times.[20] Through the activity of the Spirit certain constellations of creatures are again and again torn from certain constancies and historical processes of development in salvific ways, and led into new continuities and historical processes of development in corrective and healing manners. Through the Spirit the historical times do not only become *kairoi*, fruitful and fulfilled times. Through the Spirit God's creative powers are mediated and become known as saving and renewing powers which without interruption act upon the creatures and through the creatures. Life which already seemed dedicated to perish is renewed. Where understanding seemed impossible, a new community is created. This is not only true of inner-creaturely relations. This is also true of the relations of creatures to God and to the divine life. Through the **overcoming power of the renewing and reviving times** of the Spirit, creatures participate in God's eternal life, they are drawn into and become involved in this life.

Without faithfulness and constancy in the activity of the first mode of being of the Godhead, without clarity in the revelation of the identity and intentions of God in the second mode of being the reviving and renewing forces of the Spirit would be unrecognizable and could not be addressed. As it is, however, the dimension comes into view which Patrick Miller has presented impressively: God does not simply want to dispose of and dominate creatures. God looks for a living relation to creatures, a relation in which God is again and again invoked, persuaded, assailed and praised, asked in prayer and glorified.[21] In the search for and in asking for God's living presence, but also in the experience of this presence, we come up with a third form of time which, however, does not gain clear religious forms of expression without historical memory and cultic continuity. I would like to term this temporal form **the complex of salvific kairological times**. These times are not merely inner-historical phenomena. As John Polkinghorne has pointed out,[22] even in a 'purely cosmological' perspective certain *kairoi* can be named which are the condition of the qualified development of the universe as 'creation'.

Without the activity of the Spirit the cosmic, biological and cultural processes would remain subject to the connections which we call 'simply natural'. Without the activity of the Spirit we would not regard Christ's history as our history, it would remain foreign to us and external. The processes which bring about rhythms, continuity and security of expectations can be clearly differentiated from those which lead to new directions through unexpected success, surprising agreement and an improbable coincidence of events. Yet we have to talk of 'perichoretic connections' among them. We can state that God's creative acts are in principle each marked by the activity of the Spirit. At the same time, we have to differentiate the emphatic and explicit activity of the Spirit from God's creative and preserving activity.

Furthermore, it is important to know that not 'anything which is the case' is indebted to God's creative activity and the power of the Spirit. It is not each and every time that is automatically sustained and filled by God's eternity. There are also times which are rejected, destined to perish, 'ageing' and 'old'. This does not exclude the possibility that God can make new, creative and healing things come from them. Christian faith will, with regard to God's love revealed in Christ, even maintain that God wills no time to be left to its lostness for ever, but that without fail God is, rather, intent on continually saving all creation.

There are *three wreaths of metaphors* which we will have to reconstruct in their consistencies and interdependences, which unfold the *perichoresis of the times in eternity*. The first wreath connects the first Person or mode of being of the Trinity to the other Persons or modes. That God the creator draws the metaphors of the king, that the biblical traditions speak of God's reign, that they apply to this reign a steadfastness surpassing the continuities of cosmic powers – all this can be explained in exploring the relation of the cosmic times to the complex of historical times. The fact that at the same time this ruling on a grand scale does not diminish or destroy God's 'merciful' concern for the specific historical and individual circumstances is marked by the metaphors of the loving parent, the shepherd and others. The rationalities which connect these complex wreaths of metaphors are certainly not only determined by the temporality/eternity framework that we have just explored. But this framework allows us to overcome the almost ubiquitous vagueness with regard to the perichoresis of the three persons or modes of being of the Trinity.

The second wreath of metaphors connects Jesus Christ, his life and his history, to the cosmic dimensions of God's reign on the one side and on the other to the salvific affiliation, both with regard to situation and individual, of the kairological dimension. The great Christological titles and eschatological visions and the metaphors of the child, friend, brother, lamb offer a pluralism of interpretations which, in the light of the Trinitarian 'perichoresis', will prove to be more than a 'plurality' of religious opinions. A 'canonical' set of metaphors relates the historical dimension to the two other temporal dimensions, thus unfolding not only Christ's earthly and heavenly life but also the Trinitarian relations that make this life the revelation of the eternal God.

The third field of metaphors relates the being and working of the Holy Spirit to Christ's person and work and to the creativity of the first Person or divine mode of being. It will be important to explore why we seem not to have such a wealth of metaphors in this respect. Does creaturely reality enter here as a metaphorical space that blurs its own determination to give witness? We urgently need a detailed exploration of the sketched 'perichoresis of times' by which God's eternity becomes present in the finite. We need to explore the grammar and the rationalities of the wreaths of metaphors, their interconnections and their differentiations. In this process of exploration we shall more clearly perceive God's creative, forgiving and redeeming activity and, at the same time, we shall be able to define more clearly the Trinitarian modes of being or persons both in their differences and in their unity.

Concentration on God's eternity and God's temporality thus proves itself to be an important key to opening up and developing Trinitarian theology. In differentiated ways, it can make us understand how God involves creatures in God's actions and includes them in the divine liveliness. Over against the mere assurances that the Holy Spirit achieves this or that this happens 'in Christ', the activity of the Triune God can be described with regard to the perichoresis of times and can in part even be made clear for non-believers. Manifest reasons of sense and experience and biblical orientation can here act together. These are no bad perspectives for faith seeking understanding and for theology's dialogue with science.

Trinitarian theology has, at least so far, been a *Christian* form of relating to and speaking of God. Trinitarian theology is on the one hand able to develop a rich and differentiated way of speaking of God. On the other hand Trinitarian theology seems, as a rule, strange to Christian surroundings whose level of religious information is weak, but above all to religious persons outside the Christian tradition. Trinitarian theology has so far been the reason for the precarious special position that Christian piety and theology have among the monotheistic religions, and for the suspicion of really being a 'tritheistic' religion. We will need experiences of dialogue between the religions over quite some time to examine this attitude in self-critical ways and, as far as possible, to do away with it. In this process, the dialogue between the churches and Israel will be of overall importance, the exchange of knowledge about perceptions of differentiations in God common to and different for Israel and the churches. Israel's differentiation between God and God's Spirit as well as between God and 'God's Chosen One', but above all the meaning and rationality of the different names of God can lead not only to important questions directed to Christian Trinitarian theology, but also to its material support.[23]

We'll critically have to re-examine the jesulogical and kyriological Christologies and ask whether there are not much stronger material commonalities between Israel and the Church, for example with regard to Israel's concentration on the Torah, the fulfilment of the Torah and its messianic mediation. This means that the theologically responsible development of Trinitarian theology and its mediation and agreement in the dialogue between the churches and Israel and, beyond this, in the interreligious dialogue, is not a matter of an exchange of one or two figures of thought or of a few actually or supposedly religious experiences of evidence. The doctrine of the living God rather deals with disclosing far-reaching connections of life and knowledge.

NOTES

1. Some of the contributions to this discourse were published in an issue of *Theology Today* 55 (1998); some of the later passages of this chapter are taken from my contribution to this issue: 'God's Eternity, God's Temporality, and Trinitarian Theology', pp. 317–28.

2. Cf. Chapter 9 on this topic.

3. Karl Barth, *Church Dogmatics*, II/1, §31.3 [=KD II/1, p. 689]. T.&T. Clark, 1957.

4. Following Paul Helm, Ingolf Dalferth has characterized this difficult situation by pointing out the unhappy alternative: If the relation of the creative God to the temporal world can be grasped as temporal, then this either possibly calls into question the coherence of the concept of God and, as Dalferth puts it, thus God's existence, since God cannot be temporarily co-present in single events which in their turn are temporally ordered. God would fall into the temporal paradox of being at the same time earlier and later than God is. Or the temporal understanding of God's relation to creation calls into question the temporal structure of the world, since from God's co-presence with temporally different events the co-presence of the non-co-present, the co-presence of yesterday and tomorrow, would result. Cf. Ingolf Dalferth, 'Gott und Zeit', in

Dieter Georgi et al. (eds), *Religion und Gestaltung der Zeit*, Kampen, 1994, p. 13. Cf. also Paul Helm, *Eternal God: A Study of God Without Time*, Oxford University Press, 1988.

5. John Polkinghorne, *Science and Christian Belief/The Faith of a Physicist*, SPCK/ Princeton University Press, 1994, p. 59.

6. Cf. Barth, *Church Dogmatics*, II/1, §31.3 [=KD II/1, p. 720, see also pp. 700ff., with reference to Augustine's exegesis of the psalms].

7. Dalferth, 'Gott und Zeit', p. 15; quotation: H. Theissing, *Die Zeit im Bild*, Wiss. Buchgesellschaft, 1987, p. 8. Translation M.W.

8. Cf. J. T. E. McTaggart, 'The Unreality of Time', *Mind* 17 (1908), pp. 457ff.

9. James Barr, *Biblical Words For Time*, SCM Press, 1962, esp. pp. 105ff.

10. Cf. Norbert Elias, 'Über die Zeit', in M. Schröter (ed.), *Arbeiten zur Wissenssoziologie 2*, Suhrkamp, 1988.

11. Dalferth, 'Gott und Zeit', pp. 18ff.

12. Cf. the helpful differentiation between a 'minimalist' and a 'maximalist' concept of 'eternity' in Ted Peters, *God as Trinity: Relationality and Temporality in Divine Life*, Westminster/John Knox Press, 1993, pp. 146ff.

13. Cf. M. Welker, 'Creation: Big Bang or the Work of Seven Days?', *Theology Today* 52 (1995), pp. 173–87; and *Creation and Reality: Theological and Biblical Perspectives*, Warfield Lectures 1991, Fortress Press, 1999, ch. 1.

14. Cf. my discussion with John Polkinghorne on these issues, particularly in Chapters 5 and 6.

15. It has been emphasized that the proper place for a Trinitarian theology is doxology: the transition from the concentrated silence before God to the joyful and grateful, enthusiastic and glorifying adoration. I learned this first from Dietrich Ritschl (*Zur Logik der Theologie. Kurze Darstellung der Zusammenhänge theologischer Grundgedanken*, Kaiser, 1984, pp. 178ff. and 336 ff.). From Patrick D. Miller I learned that a complementary discovery is needed, namely that Trinitarian theology is to be located, too, in lamentation, in public petitionary prayer and in the common quest after God's justice (theodicy). (Cf. his book: *They Cried to the Lord: The Form and Theology of Biblical Prayer*, Fortress Press, 1994, pp. 68ff. and 262ff.) This means that we have to take seriously God's liveliness, the divine revelation and the creative action not only in times and situations of life which are good, happy and freeing, but also in situations of life that are unhappy, enslaving and crying for salvation and redemption. If we want to take the Triune God seriously, we have to discover as *Sitz im Leben* of Trinitarian theology also prayer and invocation in crises and emergencies, in the forms of lament, and the question of theodicy.

16. Cf. Chapter 2, and Welker, *Creation and Reality*, ch. 3.

17. W. Pannenberg, *Systematische Theologie*, vol. 1, Vandenhoeck, 1988, pp. 121ff.

18. Cf. Welker, *Creation and Reality*, ch. 2. William Stoeger has drawn attention to the fact that vague perspectives on the unity and directedness of natural laws try to pursue this idea of God which disregards God's revelation in Christ and in the activity of the Holy Spirit.

19. Cf. Friedrich Cramer, *Der Zeitbaum. Grundlegung einer allgemeinen Zeittheorie*, Insel, 1996, esp. pp. 61ff.
20. Cf. with regard to the 'pouring' of the Spirit, M. Welker, *God the Spirit*, trans. John Hoffmeyer, Fortress Press, 1994, pp. 147ff. and 228ff.
21. Patrick D. Miller, 'Prayer and Divine Action', in Tod Linafelt and Timothy Beal (eds), *God in the Fray: A Tribute to Walter Brueggemann*, Fortress, 1998.
22. 'Natural Science, Temporality, and Divine Action', *Theology Today* 55 (1998), pp. 329ff.
23. It was Moshe Idel who opened my eyes to the possibilities of an interreligious discourse on the living God, which has to take seriously a differentiation in God that many speculative and metaphysical God-thoughts try to avoid. This book can be understood as a step in this direction.

9

THE SEARCH FOR TRUTH AND UNDERSTANDING

JOHN POLKINGHORNE AND MICHAEL WELKER

Two authors have given outlines of how they understand faith in the Triune God. One writes from an academic background in theoretical physics and with a sustained concern for how the scientific and theological views of reality relate to each other. The other author is a systematic theologian who has consistently displayed sensitivity to the insights of cultural studies and also paid careful attention to questions raised by philosophy. Part of the interest in our contributions lies, we believe, in their providing an example of how two people with such differing backgrounds approach central theological questions relating to the Christian faith that they both share. That there are many contrasts between us is easy enough to see, and it is partly brought out in the brief comments that each has appended to the work of the other. Yet there is also a significant degree of commonality beneath the surface of the discussion, arising from a basic similarity of approach on both our parts to how the search for truth and understanding should be undertaken. In particular, we both seek to give full weight to the indispensable insights of the biblical traditions.

Faith and Knowledge

The life of faith demands both a scrupulous search for truth and also a humble recognition of the limitations of the human intellect when it seeks to wrestle with the infinite Reality of God. Both aspects are important. The former without the latter could only lead to the hubris of rational overconfidence and encourage the error of oversimplification; the latter without the former could lead only to agnostic despair or fideistic assertion. We would both concur with Michael Welker's statement that 'Faith is a ground for commitment, and a questioning of our commitments; faith includes reliable knowledge, and at the same time it is an awareness of the limits of knowledge.'

Our concern is with reliability but it cannot be with simple certainty. It seems clear that the twentieth century showed us that certainty, in some absolute sense, is both very scarce and only attainable in situations too trivial to make it worth having. Kurt Gödel demonstrated that even mathematics has an inescapable degree of logical uncertainty, in that it cannot yield an inexorable deduction of all that is stateable, derived from axioms that are known to be consistent. The life of faith, carefully construed, is the rational life both in science and in theology, but in neither can it be a life of absolute certainty.

Critical and Self-Critical Realism

Both authors are committed to the stance of critical realism, that is to say, to a belief that the aim of enquiry is to attain an understanding conformed to the way things actually are. That is why, for us, religious faith is primarily concerned with the Reality of God. We encounter that Reality as it is made known to us in the gracious gift of the divine presence, eliciting in its turn a human response. That response involves the whole person, going far beyond the mere assent of the intellect, although, of course, including that assent. There are both subjective and objective dimensions to the experience. Involved are the gracious movement of God towards the creature and the obedient and worshipful movement of the creature towards God. Both the givenness of the divine, and also the human response that is an essential aspect of true reception of that gift, are illustrated by the story of Isaiah's vision in the Temple (Isaiah 6). The prophet beholds the Lord 'high and lifted up', the centre of the heavenly worship of the Seraphim. This overwhelming experience of numinous presence is the given fact that calls forth the human response of Isaiah, acknowledging first his sinfulness, and the communal sin of his people Israel, and then receiving the cleansing that enables him to accept the divine call to his prophetic vocation.

Consequences of religious faith for individual styles of life, and for community living, are of great value and importance, but in themselves they are secondary in their character, for they are not what the principal concern of doctrine is about (as if it were a disguised strategy to encourage ethical behaviour). But neither is doctrine principally about propositional knowledge stated in some prosaic and itemized way, since the transpersonal divine Reality is not to be caught in such rational nets. As we have already said, the central concern of doctrine is with the Reality of God. So great a subject might seem daunting to human finitude, and it is true that theology must always be aware of its necessarily apophatic dimension. Its discourse must include making use of the open resources of metaphor and symbol, by means of which the truth of God may be affirmed without its grandeur and depth being diminished.

Already in the case of science, the adjective 'critical' in relation to the realist quest is an indispensable qualification, for it signifies that verisimilitude, rather than absolute truth, will be the outcome of the endeavour, and that the method by which it is sought will be too subtle to be reduced to the following of some specifiable protocol. Acts of judgement will be required that call upon the tacit skills that human beings are found to possess and to be able to exercise with care, while not being able to spell out completely how they do so. There is also an inescapable degree of circularity, as one seeks to believe in order to understand, without abandoning the need for understanding as the rational basis for motivated belief.[1] All these provisos made about scientific method apply with greatly increased relevance to theology's search for truth.

The philosopher of science who has most clearly made this plain is Michael Polanyi.[2] He is able both to recognize science's logical precariousness and yet to defend its actual success. Polanyi does so by reference to those tacit skills that he believes are to be learnt within the practice of a truth-seeking community, and which are subsequently to be exercised with universal intent. The relevance of all this to the much more difficult and demanding task of theology is clear enough. It cannot truly be pursued without a commitment of faith, but to say that is not to condemn theologians to life in a fideistic ghetto.

From Experience to Understanding

A second point of similarity between us is that we both are wary of generalizing abstractions, and therefore we seek to anchor our thought in concrete particulars. John Polkinghorne calls this 'bottom-up thinking',[3] the attempt to move from experience to understanding. By appeal to experience is by no means meant a Baconian accumulation of particular instances, assembled in the hope of eventually making an inductive leap. Experience and interpretation will always intertwine in hermeneutic circularity, but one should try to make the circles as tight and as small as possible. Bottom-up thinking is an instinctive stance for a scientist to adopt. Study of the physical world has shown us many surprises (quantum theory is, perhaps, the outstanding example). In consequence, scientists are loath to give much credence to *a priori* or transcendental notions of what is reasonable. Experience often breaks the mould of our prior expectation, and so we have to be open and humble enough to submit to the way things actually are. Once again, one can see how absolutely essential this stance is also to theology, lest it should succumb to the temptation to turn its current idea of God into an unrevisable idol.

In their quests for understanding, both science and theology have to speak of *unseen realities*, whether they be the quarks and gluons of elementary particle physics or the invisible Reality of God. Both have, therefore, to defend such a belief against the criticisms of a positivistic scepticism. Both can do so in essentially similar terms, basing their cases on an appeal to *intelligibility*. It is because the assumption of the existence of quarks and gluons makes sense of great swathes of physical experience, which otherwise would be opaque to us, that physicists believe in their existence, despite the fact that current physical orthodoxy assures them that these constituents are 'confined' and they will never be open to even indirect individual inspection. It is because belief in the Triune God makes sense of great swathes of spiritual experience, both that recorded in the New Testament and that known to the succeeding generations of Christian believers, that Christians are able to embrace the faith expressed in the Nicene Creed.

Bottom-up thinkers are epistemologically pragmatic, in the sense that they are not disposed to believe in the existence of a universal method, but instead they seek to tailor their approach according to the nature of particular reality as it is apprehended. Some theologians seem to be so greatly concerned with the discussion of general methodological strategy that it can preclude their ever getting down to the consideration of specific issues. The two authors greatly prefer a kind of improvisatory approach, in which the topic itself is allowed to shape the way in which it is discussed. We are suspicious of 'the Emperor's New Method', of any claim to have found a key that will turn the locks of every door in the house of theological knowledge.

Trinitarian Belief

In our mutual interaction, we have been greatly concerned with questions of theological content. Both of us believe that it is only a theological position that is fully Trinitarian that will have a content rich enough to afford a fully persuasive basis for Christian faith. Science has found that there are many surprises awaiting us in our exploration of the physical world, which cause us to revise our 'common-sense' modes of thought. Theology may reasonably be expected to be at least as mentally expansive.

This point of view is exactly the opposite of what is commonly supposed to be the case. The popular idea seems to be that a pallid deism is easy to swallow, because it makes so little demand for change from everyday thinking, while adopting a Trinitarian faith would be bizarre, requiring the embrace of the incredible and mystifying. The preceding chapters of Part I have sought to explain why we repudiate this position. We both seek an understanding of God that is not absolute and abstract, but rooted in the rich experience of Israel and the Church and principally manifested neither in 'the starry heavens above' nor in 'the moral law within', but in the person of Jesus Christ, crucified and risen.

In consequence, we both share a desire to take the *biblical witness* of the Old and New Testaments with the utmost seriousness. Of course, this does not commit us to a fundamentalist sense of the 'inerrancy' of Scripture. In the pages of the Bible we find both eternally open truths and culturally confined perspectives. Great subtleties are involved in working out what a truth-seeking biblical faithfulness involves, but it is a task to which we are both committed. John Polkinghorne greatly values Michael Welker's bonding of exegetical concerns with systematic theological insights. The discussion of the 'two times' of Genesis 1 is an illustration of the fruitfulness of this approach. Once again one encounters the need for bottom-up thinking, for this interactive strategy is one that must be developed in relation to individual passages of Scripture and it cannot be reduced to the following of one master method of exegesis.

Yet are not science and cultural studies very different backgrounds to theological thought? That is obviously the case, but we both share a strong desire to take seriously the insights arising from the other's sphere of expertise. There are many reasons that encourage a scientist to adopt this stance.

The Perspective of the Scientist

One, of course, is simply that scientists are people and their personal lives have a richness and depth to them that is missing from the lunar landscape described by science's impersonal account. There is very much more to say than an impoverished scientism could ever articulate. Many scientists take culture seriously and value it greatly but, at the end of the day, some of them see it as no more than a human construct. There are a great variety of human cultures, just as there are a great variety of human languages (there are obvious connections between the two). The extreme postmodernist will claim that diverse languages reflect the diverse linguistic usages of different communities, but they are not channels of reference to reality. The number of different colour words in a community's language may tell us about how its members organize their perception of the world, but it does not reflect intrinsic properties of the electromagnetic spectrum. Pushing such cultural relativism to its limits has led some to give a strong sociological account of science, concluding that most of its claimed insights are just agreements by the invisible college to see things that way.

Almost all scientists repudiate this view. Nature resists our prior expectation, surprising us time and again and reinforcing the conviction that scientific investigation is a process of discovery. Scientists, therefore, invoke a saving clause in their own defence, but they are more prone to take a constructivist view of other cultural activities. It is absolutely central to our critical realist position to resist this relativizing tendency. We both want to work within the concept that *all* forms of human experience and enquiry are to be taken seriously, on their proper terms and in the widest possible way, as opening a series of windows onto reality. These openings offer us a variety of perspectives that all need to be taken into account in forming our understanding of the one reality to which they give access. Science's story of the wonderful rational order of the physical world, and the unfolding fruitfulness of its history, must be combined with our experience that this same world is also the carrier of beauty, the arena of moral choice and responsibility, and the vehicle of encounter with the presence of the divine.

Thus, we both affirm a principle of the *plenitude of experience*, but not a principle of simple credulity, for one must inspect with care the view from each such window and ask whether its perspective may not involve distortion as well as insight. Given such carefulness, the aim is then to place Christian thought within the context of such a generous and comprehensive metaphysic.

Integration

There is a concept which can provide a common meeting ground for the insights of both science and cultural studies. Chapter 7 introduced the idea of active information from a scientific point of view. A suitably rich and powerful concept of information-content, relating to the creation and sustaining of novel pattern, can cover the emergence of fertile structures both in the physical world and also within the life of a truth-seeking religious community.

If we define reality as 'what we bump into' – in other words, what we encounter that demands our attention and what authenticates itself in our engagement with it – then a capacious and 'thick' account of reality is alone adequate to human experience. We are both believers in the unity of knowledge. One of the attractions of theology is that it strongly encourages the search for such an integrated view of reality. The scientist's discovery of the rationally beautiful fundamental order of the universe is a discernment of the mind of the creator. Our ethical intuitions are intimations of the perfect divine will, and our aesthetic delight is a sharing in the joy of creation. Religious experience is response to the divine presence. In this way, faith is able to integrate what otherwise would seem to be puzzlingly unrelated aspects of human encounter with reality.

Knowledge will be found to be one because God is one. Yet this unity is not to be brought about by a kind of obsessive tidiness that tries to achieve premature order by the Procrustean technique of cutting off what does not immediately fit in. Indeed, the experienced otherness of God warns us against the temptation to believe that a grand synthesis is readily within our intellectual grasp. We must take the apophatic aspect of theology seriously, without allowing ourselves to be reduced to total silence. The bottom-up thinker, despite an ultimate conviction of the unity of knowledge, has often to be satisfied pragmatically with something of a piecemeal search for understanding, made all the more necessarily tentative by the very richness of the reality that it is sought to embrace. One of the virtues of wrestling with the biblical tradition is that its variety reflects something of the many-levelled character of creation. John Polkinghorne wrote that 'I feel I must try to use each part of the scriptures in a way that proves possible and appropriate for it. Only then would the untidiness yet hopefulness of life find its match in the untidiness yet hopefulness of scripture.'[4]

Science is a matter for experts, and its advance is critically dependent on the insights of the men and women of genius. Although theological reflection itself, in its academic mode, may also be a matter for experts, it draws its material from the tradition as it is lived out by the holy common people of God. Among that community are the saints and mystics whose testimonies bear witness to profound encounters with the divine, but there is also a tradition, particularly preserved and respected in the Eastern Church, that the ultimate test of theological insight is its reception by the whole community of the faithful. The deeply personal experience that is the foundation of religious faith, cannot be reduced to a standard pattern, but neither is it so idiosyncratic that it is subject to no form of constraint or test of its validity.

For many Christians, the prime expression of their spiritual life is worship within the eucharistic liturgy of the Church. Liturgy provides a common framework that both contains and enables the individual responses of the worshippers, taking place within the common life of the gathered community of the faithful. It affords a pattern within which the search for truth by the bottom-up thinker, seeking an honest, open and adequate response to the reality and Reality within which we live, can also find a place.

Theology and the Search for Truth: The Most Basic Form of Theology[5]

This book, written for troubled friends and educated despisers of Christianity, wants to encourage its readers to join us in serious theological thinking about the living God. Not every remark about God is theological. On closer consideration, not even every pious utterance can be considered theological. The sigh directed to God and the silent prayer are no more theological utterances than the cynical remark about God or the presentation, consciously carried out under the rubric of religious studies, which makes clear that it is talking about a religion that is spiritually profoundly foreign to the speaker.

In order for an utterance to be acknowledged as theological, at least two things must be present.

First, a theological utterance about God or about matters religious does not have to evidence a well-developed 'faith', but – to put it cautiously – it *must show a minimum of conviction and a minimal degree of having been existentially influenced.* If this is not expressly true for the speaker, it at least needs to be true for the subject matter of the statement: for example, with regard to believers who are under discussion in their speaking about God. No matter what the reflective distance may be at which faith appears in theological utterances, if those utterances do not evidence a minimum of certainty shared or valued by the speaker, if they do not at least evidence the search for spiritual reliability and truth or the need to believe, then these statements about God and matters religious cannot be considered theological. Let us say explicitly: this is only the first of two conditions. On its own it is insufficient. But even the fulfilment of this condition does not go without saying in all utterances that claim to be theological. Members of church communities sometimes find this condition inadequately met in parts of academic theology.

The second presupposition is no less demanding. A theological utterance *must be formulated in words and must be comprehensible. It must be such that others can follow its logic, and it must be capable of material development.* In order to reach the level of *theological propositions*, religious utterances must express certainties that are communicable, comprehensible and open to development with respect to their object and content. Academic theology sometimes finds this side underdeveloped in church life. Again and again there are individual religious utterances that not only remain self-enclosed, but want to remain that way: hermetic certainties that do not allow either comprehension or connection. Such utterances – worthy of esteem as they may otherwise be – also do not satisfy the minimal conditions for being theological.

Thus we already have an important result: Propositions about God can certainly be fragmentary, rudimentary and distanced, and yet still be theological. However, they need to evidence an existential seriousness and a comprehensible treatment of content and subject matter in order to satisfy the minimal conditions for being theological. This reveals a fascinating basic constitution of what it is to be theological. *In speaking about God, theology connects and interrelates consistency of conviction and consistency of subject matter.* Theology does not look only for certainty and consensus. Nor does it look only for correctness and accuracy. *In the search for certainty, consensus, accuracy and correctness, theology asks for truth: that is, for the connection and mutual enhancement of consistency of conviction and consistency of subject matter in speech about God.*

Once this inner constitution of what is theological is recognized, we can value as theological even fragmentary utterances that we find in church communities and in the public outside the Church – and not only among so-called laity and outsiders. We can also acknowledge as theological very distanced utterances about God that we encounter, for instance, in some historical and philosophical academic theologies. We can accept as theological what is fragmentary, distanced and implicit, without blurring the boundary separating utterances that are not theological, or not yet theological.

Thus we call statements about God and other contents of faith theological if they show an existential seriousness in the speaker and/or in the subject matter, and if at the same time they are comprehensible, communicable and capable of material development. We presuppose this concept of theology when we say that all members of the Church, all members of the body of Christ, are able to do theology. And it is this form of theology that we also find – more or less cultivated – in public spheres outside the communities of faith.

This minimal (but at the same time sophisticated and demanding!) definition of theology is easily lost from sight because frequently we understand theology as *talk about God in a highly developed inter-connection between thought and conviction.*

Theology and the Search for Truth: Blessings and Potential Dangers of Elaborated Forms of Theology

We see a well-elaborated interconnection of thought and conviction when we speak, for instance, of the theology of Calvin or Barth, the theology of the Lutheran confessional writings, the theology of a biblical book, or the theology of a mature religious person (who need not be a learned person). We see a well-elaborated interconnection of thought and conviction when we speak of the theology of a dogmatics, a congregation, or a church tradition. As a rule such elaborated theologies do not arise outside communities of faith. Even where they are developed by individuals, they presuppose religious movements, congregations, churches and church education, and in all this, tradition and intense spiritual exchange.

Whereas in all theological utterances the consistency of conviction and subject matter and their connection and mutual enhancement may only be latently present, in elaborated theologies we find them developed and verified. The verification of elaborated theologies in diverse questions of certainty, correctness and truth is a great good. Communities of faith are shaped by such theologies. Explicit theologies, which have taken shape in confessions and confessional writings, in catechisms and textbooks, in hymnody and liturgies, mark communities of faith. But so do implicit theologies, which in the living processes of teaching, proclamation and spiritual discourse often find only fragmentary expression and are continually being developed. Major communities of faith with a long tradition are shaped by a whole hierarchy of theologies, which must be essentially compatible with each other, or which must be the subject of ongoing debate with regard to their compatibility. In this context one can speak of 'a' or 'the' theology of a community of faith, although the unity of this theology often becomes clearly accessible only in conflict, in the formation of confessions, in ordination vows, and in other limited situations.

In light of the great value of the elaborated theologies that shape a community of faith, people often overlook the fact that elaborated theologies can become degenerate and deformed. Not just fragmentary theological utterances, but highly developed theologies and interconnections of theological reflection can prove to be false and deceptive. To be sure, every theology aims at certainty, correctness and truth. But no theology has a monopoly on the truth or its full possession.

For this reason elaborated theologies are not in themselves a blessing. They can have devastating consequences, although they were developed and defended with the best of intentions. We know that highly consistent, long-recognized theologies can undergird, transport and export bad ideologies. They may even become ideologies themselves. Precisely because elaborated theologies can acquire major formative influence, they can contribute not only to the strengthening, but also to the severe distortion of faith.[6] Today it is part of the familiar form of theological self-criticism to acknowledge that for centuries Christian theologies have supported patriarchal, chauvinistic, classist and imperialistic attitudes. Moreover, we are beginning to see particularly that neo-Protestant theologies, by mixing and confusing faith with an empty religious certainty, have contributed to a systematic emptying out and individualization of religion in Christian churches. At the beginning of the third millennium, the classical mainline churches in the Western industrialized nations suffer greatly from this problem.

We gain access to this complicated constellation when we see that there is a third sense in which we speak of theology and theologies. In this third sense we do not refer merely to a *fragmentary intellectual and epistemic theological initiative,* or merely to an *elaborated interconnection of thought,* but to a *process* that mediates between these two extremes. More precisely, we refer to a multiplicity of intellectual and epistemic processes that move back and forth between the two poles named above. These intellectual and epistemic processes become particularly clear in *academic theology.* For this reason many people equate theology and academic theology. However, this is not correct. To be sure, a relatively long period of education is necessary to become familiar with one or even several elaborated theologies, to penetrate them, to subject them to critical comparison, and to examine and test them. Such an education is hardly possible unless one's studies and vocation provide one the freedom to pursue it. But a mere occupation with well-elaborated theologies can miss the decisive task of theology, if that occupation does not serve to promote both existential access to faith and also the unfolding of the subject matter of faith, thereby serving to enhance theological labour 'from below'. This *theological labour 'from below',* which can – but need not – aim at a comprehensive systematic theology, is by no means the privilege of academic theology alone. It is the task of every Christian – indeed in communities of faith outside of Christianity it is the task of every religious person – who wants to understand faith and who thereby confronts the question of truth.

As soon as religious persons express themselves as such in content-related ways about God and their faith, are understood, and spur other persons to new and further utterances about God, there is also theology in public settings outside communities of faith. However, it is improbable that theologies in the sense of comprehensive interconnections of thought and conviction be elaborated in this way, unless communities of faith make themselves known or public religions become communities of faith. And the reflected co-presence of diverse elaborated theologies is sure to remain restricted to communities of faith and to theological institutions of education and research.

Five Forms of Religious Minimalism as Dangerous Bridges Between Elaborated and Basic Theologies

There have again and again been attempts to develop or to diagnose minimalist religious forms of thought supposed to be decisive for large societal groupings, in order to be able to specify in this way an apparently comprehensive theology for large public groupings outside communities of faith. This theme has been the subject of intensive discourse under the heading of 'civil religion'. In the nineteenth and twentieth centuries in the sphere of influence of the mainline Christian churches we can observe at least five forms that have shaped not only the theologies within communities of faith, but also religious mentalities and the capacity for theological expression beyond the confines of those communities.

The first of these forms is *classical* abstract *theism* with its belief in God as a transcendent agent or personality who brought forth and defines himself and everything else.[7] This theism has found expression in formulae such as God as the 'ultimate point of reference' (Gordon Kaufman), God as the 'ground of being' (Paul Tillich and others), God as 'first cause' (in many popular conceptions of creation), and God as the 'whence of our absolute dependence' (Friedrich Schleiermacher). Second, a *religious holism* has repeatedly been put forward that always presumes there is a relation to God and to religious themes whenever the conversation turns to 'the whole' and to any form of 'wholeness'. Third, we find abundant *forms of religiously imbued moralism*, be they conservative or progressive. Religious thought specifies itself in a spectrum of particular moral expectations and demands, and moral communication gains emphasis through an accompanying religious tone – a religious 'second coding', as some sociologists say.

In the twentieth century two further forms inside and outside communities of faith have had a great effect: namely, religious dialogism or personalism, and existentialism. It is remarkable that *religious dialogism* has flourished with the introduction of electronic mass media and totalitarian states, on the one hand, and with the emergence of pluralistic societies, on the other. Religious dialogism sees the relation between God, human beings and creation as an intimate 'I–Thou relation', and attempts (in vain) to articulate all religious matters in this form. Influential Jewish thinkers like Martin Buber, and leading representatives of so-called dialectical theology like Karl Barth and Emil Brunner, have contributed both indirectly and directly to the fact that dialogism has at times overshadowed moralism and existentialism as a theological form of thought in church and culture.

Finally, however, *religious existentialism* has become still more influential, especially in public settings outside communities of faith. Existentialism draws the theistic God or the great 'Thou' of dialogism completely into interiority and self-reference. 'God' is the 'other' in me, in my innermost certainty. This form has become extremely powerful. It has put itself forward as the purest faith, as pure certainty that takes particularly seriously God's ineffability and God's proximity to every human being. *In actual fact this form can become the death of theology, because it reduces faith to mere inner certainty and deprives it of content and the capacity for expression and communication.* With compelling logic, this religious form destroys theological communication inside and outside communities of faith. On the one hand, it seems to open rapid and immediate access to God in the same way for every person: Go inside yourself and your feelings, and you will find an 'other' in yourself that stands over against you, yet at the same time is infinitely familiar to you. But in truth this form only draws attention to empty certainty and self-certainty as such. It puts an end to theological communication where it apparently begins.

Faith in the Living God: Theology in Search for Truth and Understanding Needs Exemplary Orientation Toward its Subject Matter

Theology has a pressing need to increase its competence in societal and cultural criticism. This increased competence does not come about by theology simply taking over a specific theory of culture and society. Within communities of faith, theology must heighten its sensitivity to the fact that human beings do not develop theological convictions and questions free from the influence of the environment, subsystems and associations in which they live, in which they commit themselves to action, and by which they are normatively shaped. Theology must also awaken a critical and self-critical sensitivity to these environmental influences. These normative powers separate and alienate human beings from one another. Whoever is defined primarily by family life and by questions of education will develop a different world view, and a differently coloured piety, than the person who is occupied on a daily basis with judicial problems or with politics. The person who lives on a daily basis primarily with the rationalities of the market and the media will be occupied with still different questions. At the same time, these normative powers bind human beings together across epochs, traditions and cultures. Theology is faced here with a whole sheet of tasks in self-education and the education of others, if it does not wish its words and its deeds to be increasingly beside the point with regard to public discourse outside communities of faith.

But what preserves theology within communities of faith, in this effort to increase their competence in societal and cultural criticism, from being diverted from their actual content and object, and from losing sight of speech about God? This question cannot be answered universally, but only for specific communities of faith. The theologies of the Christian communities of faith have been given an excellent basis on which to school their familiarity with speech about God in an abundance of contexts, both in their differences and in their interconnections. The biblical traditions, which developed over a period of more than 1,000 years, offer an abundance of contexts with very different exemplary existential, moral, political and cultural misfortunes and adversities in which faith in God has been formulated and communicated. From the Exodus to Paul's political sensibility, the biblical traditions document theologically oriented life precisely in interaction with diverse 'situations in life'. From the presentation of creation as the interdependence of cosmic, biological, cultural and religious processes, by way of the numerous reflections on the conflict-laden relations between Israel and the nations, Jews and Gentiles, and the Church and Israel, to the description of the Church as the body of Christ with many members and to the logic of the 'pouring out of the Spirit', we encounter an abundance of creative theological content and forms that must repeatedly be rediscovered. A theology schooled in biblical theology will develop and practice the sensitivity to discriminate good simplifications from deceptive ones, necessary ways of rendering something plausible from false populism, indispensable concentration and clarity from bad reductionism.

Over and over again it happens that when theology takes its orientation from the biblical traditions, reductionistic systematic forms to which theology is captive both inside and outside communities of faith are broken open. Abstract theism, dialogism and existentialism must face the question of whether and to what extent they are really speaking of a loving creator and of God's creativity, whether they are able to cast light on the divinity of the risen Christ, whether they make it possible to talk about the divinity of the Holy Spirit, and – throughout it all – whether they enable people to call upon, honour, experience and think the Triune God. Dogmatically, we need a renewed understanding of the living God – an understanding that, in the perception of many persons today, classical theism has hindered more than helped. But there is also a pressing necessity for a differentiated understanding of the word of God that makes it possible to bring the various dimensions (Christ as the one Word of God, sacred Scripture as God's word, God's word in the form of law and gospel) into a consistent interconnection.[8]

Over against all versions of reductionistic generalization theology must continually seek to awaken delight in the specificity of faith's content. It must set an example by cultivating mentalities and forms in which both the certainty of faith, and delight in faith's focus on its content and subject matter, not only are wakened but, on the basis of the question of truth, mutually challenge and stimulate each other. This occurs in the discursive process of coming to theological understanding. It sounds strange to demand that theology should cultivate discursive theological understanding. But this demand stands in conflict with systematic and practical theologies that, usually unintentionally, work toward holding people in theological immaturity, both inside and outside communities of faith. Which kinds of theology contribute to keeping people theologically immature? One can rightly point to theologies that condemn 'the laity' merely to listen to 'the teaching Church' or, put more mildly, release them from their theological responsibility. One can also point to theologies that, working from a generalizing mentality, deform and undermine both faith's certainty and its focus on its content and subject matter. With monohierarchical patterns of thought, with dualistic images of the world, with an ethos reaching no further than the realm of 'I and Thou', with vague moralisms, and with an equally vague rhetoric of plurality, numerous theologies have contributed to the situation where faith, if it dares at all to express itself publicly, simply talks past contemporary culture and a halfway-educated common sense. Changing this state of affairs is one of the primary tasks of the theology that proceeds from communities of faith.

But what is the guiding conception that can replace a bad orientation toward religious minimalism? The struggle for an *exemplary orientation toward its subject matter* is the distinctive mark of a theology arising from communities of faith which in the future can exercise a beneficial influence in public discourse outside communities of faith. Without surrendering the high esteem for personal certainty of faith, theology must learn to discover, and teach others to discover, faith's power to provide insight and understanding in respect of the contents of faith. This exemplary orientation to theology's subject matter must prove itself both in turning to the decisive testimonies of the tradition, and also in sensitive engagement with the burning questions posed by our contemporary cultures and societies.

NOTES

1. Cf. discussions in J. C. Polkinghorne, *Beyond Science*, Cambridge University Press, 1996, ch. 2; *Belief in God in an Age of Science*, Yale University Press, 1998, ch. 5.
2. M. Polanyi, *Personal Knowledge*, Routledge and Kegan Paul, 1958.
3. J. C. Polkinghorne, *Science and Christian Belief/The Faith of a Physicist*, SPCK/ Princeton University Press, 1994.
4. Polkinghorne, *Christian Belief/Faith*, p. 153.
5. The following passages are in parts identical with Michael Welker, 'Theology in Public Discourse Outside Communities of Faith?', in *Religion, Pluralism and Public Life: Abraham-Kuyper's Legacy for the Twenty-first Century*, ed. Luis Lego, introduction by Max Stackhouse, Eerdmans, 2000.
6. Cf. Max Stackhouse, 'The Sociology of Religion and the Theology of Society', *Social Compass* 37 (1990), pp. 315–29, at p. 325: 'Of course religion can go sour and destroy social systems, just as can broken families, failed economies, violent regimes and meaningless cultural artificiality. It can, when badly formed, contribute to the destruction of these systems, just as its critics have claimed. Rotten religion can be sexually repressive, economically disfunctional, politically oppressive and culturally ugly.'
7. For a strong critique of this religious form and power see such different positions as: Karl Barth, *Church Dogmatics*, II.2; Alfred North Whitehead, *Process and Reality: An Essay in Cosmology*, Macmillan, 1927; Jürgen Moltmann, *Der gekreuzigte Gott. Das Kreuz Christi als Grund und Kritik christlicher Theologie*, 6th edn, Kaiser, 1993; Eberhard Jüngel, *Gott als Geheimnis der Welt. Zur Begründung der Theologie des Gekreuzigten im Streit zwischen Theismus und Atheismus*, 6th edn, Mohr, 1992; Michael Welker, *Creation and Reality: Theological and Biblical Perspectives*, Warfield Lectures 1991, Fortress Press, 1999.
8. Cf. Michael Welker and David Willis (eds), *Towards the Future of Reformed Theology*, Eerdmans, 1998.

INDEX